Abo

ALI BACHER was educated at King Edward VII School (captaining the 1st XI and Transvaal Nuffield XI) and Wits University, where he studied medicine. He captained Transvaal aged 21 and played 12 Tests between 1965 and 1970, when he captained South Africa to a 4-0 Test whitewash of Australia. He went on to a distinguished career in cricket administration, culminating in the hosting of the 2003 World Cup in South Africa. He is chairman of the AIDS charity Right to Care.

DAVID WILLIAMS was also educated at King Edward VII School (he played rugby for the 1st XV and Transvaal Schools) and Wits University, majoring in history, political science and English. David was deputy editor of the *Financial Mail*, and has worked extensively in radio (notably on 702 and Highveld) and television. He is now senior anchor on the daily "Business Tonight" TV programme on CNBC Africa Channel 410.

WE CELEBRATE
SOUTH AFRICA'S
GREATEST BATSMEN

BOSCHENDAL

Founded 1685

South Africa's Greatest Batsmen

South Africa's Greatest Batsmen

Past and Present

Ali Bacher and David Williams

With a chapter by Krish Reddy

PENGUIN BOOKS

Published by Penguin Books
an imprint of Penguin Random House South Africa (Pty) Ltd
Reg. No. 1953/000441/07
The Estuaries No. 4, Oxbow Crescent, Century Avenue, Century City, 7441
PO Box 1144, Cape Town, 8000, South Africa

www.penguinbooks.co.za

First published 2015

1 3 5 7 9 10 8 6 4 2

PUBLISHER: Marlene Fryer
MANAGING EDITOR: Robert Plummer
EDITOR: Alison Lowry
PROOFREADER: Pam Thornley
COVER DESIGNER: Sean Robertson
TYPESETTER: Monique van den Berg
INDEXER: Sanet le Roux

Set in 11.5 pt on 15.5 pt Adobe Garamond

Printed and bound by CTP Book Printers, Duminy Street, Parow, 7500

ISBN 978 1 77022 865 8 (print)
ISBN 978 1 77022 866 5 (ePub)
ISBN 978 1 77022 867 2 (PDF)

Contents

Authors' Note

"We have a combined 116 years of passionately following the game of cricket in South Africa."

Ali remembers going to Ellis Park in 1949 with his uncle to watch the touring Australians. "I can remember it like it was yesterday." That started a lifelong love affair with the game. Apart from Herby Taylor, he has personally known every player selected to appear in this book.

He believes that the history of South African cricket falls into two eras. "The first was from the 1880s to the 1950s. In that time we were always number three to Australia and England. We hardly had a fast bowler and our batting was always defensive. We had no Larwood, no Tyson, no Constantine. Then came Neil Adcock, Peter Heine and Peter Pollock, and our bowling began to be aggressive and effective – with a great line going through the likes of Mike Procter, Allan Donald, Makhaya Ntini and Dale Steyn. They enabled our batsmen to be aggressive and make big scores quickly."

David was aware via Charles Fortune's radio commentary on the exploits of the South African teams in Australia and England in the early 1960s, but he attended his first Test match (also with his uncle) in December 1966, when the Springboks were playing Bobby Simpson's touring Australians. Having listened to the SABC's ball-by-ball commentary on the early stages of the match on short-wave radio, he was at the Wanderers Stadium when Ali was run out for 67, in South Africa's second innings of 620.

Unlike Ali, he failed to make the grade at cricket at King Edward VII School, playing as a leg-spinner for the 4th XI; he did make his mark in other sports, winning colours in rugby and athletics. But he became devoted to cricket as a school scorer, coach and umpire, and as a broadcaster and writer on the game – and he worked for many years as the public address announcer at the Wanderers. This culminated in his being asked by Ali to organise the PA operation for the 2003 ICC Cricket World Cup in South Africa.

"We have known each other for 35 years, united by our background at a great cricketing school and our passion for the game. We have so enjoyed exploring and debating the records of our great batsmen, and sharing our conclusions."

ALI BACHER
DAVID WILLIAMS
JULY 2015

Introduction

Batsmen in Test cricket are regarded as excellent if they achieve a career average of more than 50. At the end of December 2014, of those from all countries who played at least 20 innings, only 39 men had managed to average 50 runs per innings in the 137 years since the first Test between England and Australia in 1877.

One must be cautious in comparing the statistics of batsmen from different eras. Scoring rates have risen in the last two decades. Until the post-isolation period, South African batsmen were tested mainly by the bowlers of England and Australia, and generally those two countries fielded powerful teams – especially in the 1930s and 1950s. Modern batsmen have had the opportunity to boost their statistics with matches against weak sides from Bangladesh and Zimbabwe – but have also had to deal with the pitches of the Indian subcontinent, which the old-timers did not.

Despite the variations, however, a batting average of 50+ remains the most important evidence of greatness. There are six South African batsmen who have achieved this: Dudley Nourse, Graeme Pollock, Jacques Kallis, AB de Villiers, Hashim Amla and Faf du Plessis (though the last three are still playing). This makes them automatic choices for our selection of great South African batsmen – except Du Plessis, whose career has just started.

If a 50+ average is "excellent", we can regard 45+ as "very good" (just 3 per cent of the 2794 men who had played Test cricket by the end of July 2015 had an average higher than 45) and 40+ as "good". It would be hard to argue that anyone with an average lower than 40 can be regarded as "great" – but some with an average between 40 and 45 might be seen as great for other reasons.

Greatness does not only derive from statistics, although they do provide an initial filter. In identifying the other players, we have also relied on written historical sources such as the *Wisden Cricketers' Almanack*, ESPN Cricinfo, a range of cricket books, and contemporary newspaper reports; on comments by respected individuals like Sir Donald Bradman; and on personal experience and observation.

From the generation that played between the two world wars (1918 to 1939), our first choice is Herby Taylor (Test average 40.77; career 1912–1932), said to be the only batsman capable of dealing with the Englishman Sydney Barnes, who was regarded by experts at the time (and since) as perhaps the greatest of all bowlers. Taylor's achievement of 508 runs in four Tests against England in 1913–14 at an average of 50.80 – a series in which Barnes took 49 wickets at 10.93 each – prompted *Wisden* half a century later to describe it as "the most skilful of all Test performances by a batsman".

Three other players stand out from that era: Bruce Mitchell (48.88; 1929–1949), Dudley Nourse (53.81; 1935–1951) and Eric Rowan (43.66; 1935–1951). They established themselves as formidable players in the 1930s, providing the backbone of a weak side that was usually outplayed; they lost eight years of their careers to World War II; and they remained the country's three best batsmen until they were in their forties.

The South African batting of the 1950s was generally inconsistent and defensive, against very powerful English and Australian teams. In the early 1960s, after several series that produced much negative cricket, it was seriously being asked whether South Africa deserved to have Test status.

The shift from an inherently defensive approach and the growth in national cricketing self-confidence probably began with the Springbok tour of Australia in 1963–64. This saw the emergence of Graeme Pollock (60.97; 1963–1970), whose Test average is still second on the all-time list only to that of Bradman. He was joined in the side in 1970 by Barry Richards (72.57; 1970), who played only four Tests but is universally regarded as one of the great batsmen of all time. Bradman picked Richards to open in his all-time World XI. The third player from that era is Colin Bland (49.08; 1961–1966), whose career was cut short by a knee injury when he was just 28 years old – and whose brilliant fielding tended to overshadow his achievements as a batsman.

Since readmission in 1992, the Proteas have generally been very successful – and have expected to be successful. After a few years of batting fragility in the team, Gary Kirsten (45.27; 1994–2003) and Jacques Kallis (56.10; 1995–2014) steadily established themselves as reliable and prolific performers, going on to play 267 Tests and 513 ODIs between them, and scoring 96 centuries in both forms of the game.

Kirsten and Kallis laid the foundation and provided inspiration for three world-class batsmen who came into the side in the new century: Graeme Smith, AB de Villiers and Hashim Amla. Capable of scoring quickly and heavily, confident in all conditions against all bowlers, they were the batting core of a side that twice won series victories in both England and Australia, defeated every other Test nation at some point, and reached the world number one ranking. Smith is the only South African to have scored five Test double-centuries; Amla is the first and only South African to score a triple hundred in Tests; and De Villiers is one of the most talented and spectacular batsmen ever to play the game.

Their contemporary Kevin Pietersen (47.28; 2005–2014), who had attended Maritzburg College, decided to further his career in the United Kingdom, where he is acknowledged as one of the best batsmen ever to play for England; he played a leading role in no fewer than three Ashes victories.

Another two batsmen, we decided, would be selected despite

their lack of international experience. They come from the ranks of black players who were excluded from selection for South Africa because of apartheid, but whose records in black club and provincial cricket suggested they would have been regarded as great if they had had the opportunity. Of course there is no way of proving this, but it is an important acknowledgement of the terrible damage that racial exclusion did to our sport and our country. The eminent cricket historian Krish Reddy has provided biographies of two outstanding batsmen who were lost to the global game, Ahmed Deedat and Frank Roro.

We excluded from consideration outstanding batsmen who had already featured in our previous book, *Jacques Kallis and 12 Other Great South African All-rounders*, in particular Jimmy Sinclair, Aubrey Faulkner and Eddie Barlow. The exception was Jacques Kallis himself, whose status as South Africa's greatest cricketer demanded that he be included again for assessment purely as a batsman.

PART ONE

THE TEST OF TIME

1

Herby Taylor, Bruce Mitchell, Dudley Nourse and Eric Rowan

T he old man was sitting in the back row in the south-western corner of the Wanderers press box, looking north over the ground from the Corlett Drive end. The seats around him were empty. He was neatly dressed in a light-grey, three-piece suit with white shirt and sober tie, his hands clasped on the desk in front of him as he leaned forward. Clearly he was taking a keen interest in the play, a thoughtful and mildly anxious expression on his face.

It was Thursday, 26 November 1992, the hot, still first day of the second Test between South Africa and India. The old man had reason to be concerned: the home side were in trouble at 26 for four (Jimmy Cook out for 2, Andrew Hudson 8, Kepler Wessels 5 and Peter Kirsten 0) after an hour and ten minutes of the morning's play. It was at this point that the old man was suddenly surrounded by several Indian journalists – standing next to him and behind him in the row, and facing up to him from the lower row in front of him. They spoke to him respectfully but excitedly. He appeared puzzled and slightly uncomfortable at the attention, and made courteous but brief replies to their questions as his eyes kept return-ing to the field. Hansie Cronje was coming onto the field to join Jonty Rhodes at the crease.

One of the Indian journalists – perhaps it was their great and recently retired batsman, Sunil Gavaskar, who was in the press box as an expert analyst – had recognised the neat, withdrawn old man and called the others across. They all knew who he was – most of the South African journalists clearly did not.

Bruce Mitchell was then 83 years old, but still the holder of the South African record for most Test runs scored: 3 471 at an average of 48.88. Between June 1929 and May 1949, he played in every one of South Africa's 42 Test matches.

What were the Indian journalists asking Mitchell? They might have wanted to know if he was disappointed in the negative play that characterised that 1992 series, of which much had been expected. Following the one-off Test against the West Indies earlier in the year, this was the first Test series involving South Africa since 1970 – and the first ever against India. Yet the crowds were disappointing – especially so in Durban, with its large population of Indian descent – and the captaincy on both sides was generally negative. Three of the four matches were drawn. Administrators began to realise how out of touch the South African players and public were with Test cricket, and indeed with their country's rich cricket heritage.

Those Indian journalists, steeped in statistics and interested in all cricket, might have been asking Mitchell about his role in the "Timeless Test" – the longest Test ever played. In addition to Mitchell, this match had featured two others from our selection of all-time great South African batsmen: Dudley Nourse and Eric Rowan.

The final Test of the 1938–39 home series against England was at Kingsmead. Going into the game, the visitors were leading the series 1-0 with three matches drawn, so it was decided that this one should be played to a finish. (This was the normal practice in Australia at the time, but not in South Africa. The other four Tests against England in 1938–39 had been played over four days.)

One of the English bowlers was Doug Wright, the Kent leg-spinner. He remembered that "this final Test had created a tremendous amount of interest, and large crowds of all nationalities were expected to see it. It started on Friday, March 3, 1939. Our skipper, Wally Hammond, had won the toss eight consecutive times, so it was hardly surprising that he lost this one. Alan Melville elected to bat. The overriding factor was the first-class condition of the pitch, which gave the bowlers no help."

The South African innings was opened by Melville and Pieter van der Bijl. Taking the view that time was not a factor, both were extremely cautious. There was no thought of trying to dominate the bowling, as a batsman like Don Bradman invariably did in timeless Tests. This reflected the unconfident, defensive mindset of South African cricket at that time. Van der Bijl took 45 minutes (and 33 balls) to score his first single, and three hours (and 196 balls) to hit a four.

After batting for more than two days, South Africa were all out for 530, with centuries by Van der Bijl (125 in more than seven hours) and Nourse (103 in six and a half hours, then a world record for the slowest Test century). Mitchell and Rowan made 44 runs between them.

England scored 316 all out, but there was no thought of asking them to follow on. South Africa replied with 481 all out, headed by Mitchell's 89 in three hours and 40 minutes, Van der Bijl's 97 and Melville's 103. Nourse made 25 and Rowan 0. (The batting seemed excruciatingly slow at the time, but the run rate in the South African second innings was 2.53 per six balls – a bit faster than their 2.45 in the first innings against India at the same ground 54 years later.)

"It was about this time," remembered Doug Wright, "that the *Athlone Castle* was getting ready to steam off down the east coast to Cape Town, on the way home to England. The team had expected to be on board, but as the match was still in progress, arrangements were made to travel by train to Cape Town. The captain of the *Athlone Castle*, just to let us know he was sailing, sounded three long farewell blasts on the ship's siren, as if saying, 'I'll see you in Cape Town'."

There are different versions of the travel timetable. Louis Duffus had a written tour itinerary which said the English players were scheduled to leave for Cape Town not by ship, but by train at 8.05pm on Tuesday, 7 March, which turned out to be the fifth day of the match in Durban. The final tour fixture was against Western Province in Cape Town the next weekend, but as the Durban game dragged on this was abandoned.

"We usually walked to the ground from the Royal Hotel," said Wright. "By now, we not only knew the way, but many of the shop-keepers and people living on the route. After all, it was the seventh day! A fair amount of good-humoured banter passed between us regarding the 696 runs we needed. No-one gave us the slightest chance."

Journalist Douglas Alexander was at the game. He recalled that "if the players didn't expect the match to last, the Imperial Airways (now British Airways) flying-boat crews had more faith. South African skipper Alan Melville gave his complimentary tickets to the crew turning round in Durban when the match began. They watched the first day's play and, on reaching Britain after a four-day flight across Africa and the Mediterranean, handed their tickets to the new crew flying south. They arrived back another four days later, yet still in time to see the end of the match."

Alexander has several other stories. Melville "was so accustomed to the daily routine of breakfast at the seafront hotel, followed by a drive to Kingsmead, that he looked around the dining-room sur-prised to see no teammates in sight. 'They'll be late for the ground if they don't hurry,' he complained to a waiter. 'But it's Sunday, sir,' replied the man, smiling. There was no play on Sundays in those days.

"Springbok Ken Viljoen was to remember it as the only time he needed two haircuts during a match. And the South African bowler Eric Dalton, whose leg-breaks and googlies reaped him six wickets, told of the enormous mental and physical strain as the marathon game dragged on. Some nights his wife would hear him appealing at the top of his voice in his sleep."

English hopes of victory revived when, by the end of the seventh day, they had reached 253 for one, with Paul Gibb on 78 and Bill Edrich on 107. The next day Edrich scored a double-century, and with the scoreboard on 400 for two, with 296 needed, the whole English team was saying, "We can win this match."

Going into the ninth day of play, they needed exactly 200 with seven wickets in hand. But then it was decided that the Test could not be timeless after all. The delayed train journey to Cape Town had to be undertaken on the Tuesday night, and so the ninth day of play had to be the last. Batting in "sultry and blustering" conditions, twelve days after the match began, and with the pitch finally breaking up and the light poor, any result was possible – and then rain came at tea-time, and the match had to be abandoned as a draw. In the end England fell short by 42 runs, while the South Africans needed to take five wickets.

By the turn of the 21st century, the last survivor from the two teams in the Timeless Test was fast bowler Norman Gordon. He was known as "Mobil" after the oil company, because he would slick down his hair with Vaseline. He bowled a record 738 balls in eight-ball overs at Kingsmead. "I still remember my flannels sticking to my legs as I toiled in Durban's humid March heat," he said in 2002. "The heat and humidity got to you."

Although Gordon's first Test victim was Walter Hammond, in the first Test match at the Wanderers, and he took more wickets (20) than any other bowler on either side in the series, in Durban Gordon took just one wicket for 256 runs. "Quite frankly I was bowled too much. I was noted for fantastic stamina and often bowled 10 or 15 eight-ball overs at a stretch. But I didn't lose heart – I was so crazy about cricket, I didn't get worried that I wasn't taking wickets."

In those days the players from both sides socialised a great deal during tours. During this marathon Test, Gordon and Eric Rowan dined regularly with Bill Edrich at a well-known nightclub at the Athlone Gardens Hotel in Durban North. They were obviously spotted, because during Edrich's massive double-century in the second innings, a spectator shouted: "This match wasn't lost at Kingsmead, it was lost at Athlone Gardens." Rowan later admitted that this remark "rather shook us".

The *Daily Telegraph* summed up a widespread view when it remarked that "England went so near to winning, that it seems difficult to understand why it was so necessary for them to catch a particular ship home".

When Gordon died in 2014 aged 103, he was the oldest former Test cricketer in the world and a living link with a distant past when there was no television, let alone cell-phones. Cricketers travelled by ship and train; some tours lasted more than six months.

"Travelling 12,000 miles by train," wrote Louis Duffus of the 1938–39 season, "meant many hours of sitting at the compartment window, or more at ease in the observation car that accompanied the team throughout the tour, gazing at strips of South African scenery that flashed past in a vast moving panorama. The views were best in the evenings. The flood of sunset colours flowing over distant ranges of mountains, or radiating from a horizon of bare veld, brought forth cries of admiration from Londoners and residents of northern industrial towns, whose chances of watching the fall of evening with such glowing tints were rare indeed."

It was a more leisurely age – but what has not changed, by all the accounts we have of pre-World War II cricket, is the intensity of the contests. However, for South African teams, it was the intensity of defence rather than aggression.

The Springboks, as they were known then, were as individuals often competitive against England and Australia (until 1928, these three were the only Test-playing nations), but as a team the South

Africans generally failed. Their standard of play between the world wars was below what they had achieved in the early 1900s. Between 1920 and 1950, South Africa played 65 Tests and won only five against England and none against Australia. Their only series win was in England in 1935 (1-0, with four matches drawn).

The performances of the leading batsmen of the period have to be seen in that context. As John Arlott said of the outstanding South African all-rounder Aubrey Faulkner, "all his career was spent playing teams stronger than his own".

Bruce Mitchell, Dudley Nourse and Eric Rowan were always under pressure because of the fragility of the batting around them, and from having to compensate for the uneven quality of their own side's bowling. Yet they each proved capable of sustaining long innings and of accumulating massive scores. Before 1970, only eight Test double-centuries had been scored by South African batsmen: Faulkner made one; three of them were by Nourse (201 and 231) and Rowan (236); and only one other player, Graeme Pollock, had made two double-hundreds. Eddie Barlow made 201 and Jackie McGlew 255 not out.

The Timeless Test in March 1939 was also South Africa's last for nearly ten years. "As the clouds broke over Kingsmead," wrote Louis Duffus, "a blacker storm was preparing to engulf the little world of cricket, as well as lands where stumps are never pitched. It was the last Test match of a troubled age. Perhaps just as well. International games were going awry. Wickets were too good and batsmen unadventurous. Some big upheaval was needed to restore the robust spirit of big cricket."

When Test cricket did resume after World War II, it was significant that for at least a decade no younger South African batsman achieved the stature of the veterans Mitchell, Nourse and Rowan. South Africa had no choice but to continue to rely on them. Between 1935 and 1951, South Africa played 35 Tests in seven series: at least two of these three batsmen played together in all 35 of them; in 15 Tests all three were selected. It is a remarkable record over 17 years, six of them lost to war. And none of the three players had declined in capacity when they retired – they were all in their 40s, but in each case there was evidence that they had more to give South African cricket. They set the standard, demonstrating South Africa's capacity to produce world-class players – if not, at that stage, world-class teams.

But before we examine their careers in more detail, there is an earlier great player whose story must be told.

Bruce Mitchell started his career in 1929 and in 13 of the first 16 of his 42 Tests, he played alongside Herby Taylor – the one outstanding South African batsman of the second and third decades of the 20th century, continuing the line established earlier by the likes of Aubrey Faulkner and Jimmy Sinclair.

Writing in the 1980s, John Arlott judged that Taylor "must be nearly the finest batsman ever produced by South Africa. He was like Jack Hobbs in the completeness of his technique. Invariably sound in his judgement of length, his footwork was neat and fast, though unhurried. Perfectly balanced, he was strong on both sides of the wicket, and he had every stroke, using them all generously."

To measure the quality of Herby Taylor's batting, we have to look at the bowling he had to deal with – in particular, one of the greatest bowlers of all time, Sydney Barnes. In the 1913–14 series between England and South Africa, Barnes took 49 wickets in four Tests at 10.93 each. This is the best bowling performance in any series in history – and it was against a South African batting order that was regarded at the time as moderately strong, and on the matting wickets that were familiar to the home side.

In Barnes's 27 Tests against South Africa and Australia, he took 189 wickets at 16.43 – the best average in history for any bowler who played 20 or more Tests. In 1929, when he was 57, he played for Staffordshire against the 1929 South African tourists –

Herby Taylor: the only man who mastered the most dangerous bowling of all

and they described him as the best bowler they encountered on the entire tour.

Neville Cardus described Barnes as "the most dangerous bowler of them all, living or dead ... on matting he made a cricket ball spit fire, gyrate and describe angles unknown to geometry". And he was aggressive, said Cardus: "a chill wind of antagonism blew from him on the sunniest day". Sir Pelham Warner wrote: "Barnes has every attribute of a great bowler. He brings the ball down from a great height, he breaks both ways, he keeps a perfect length, and finally his flight is most deceptive. His leg-break is not only accurate, but very quick off the pitch."

Only one man mastered Barnes in that 1913–14 series: Herby Taylor. He made 508 runs in the Tests at an average of 50.80 – "perhaps," said *Wisden* half a century later, "the most skilful of all Test performances by a batsman". Arlott believed that his performance in 1913–14 "was utterly outstanding, against what was by common contemporary consent the most dangerous bowling of all – that of SF Barnes on a matting wicket".

"Barnes was a marvellous bowler," Taylor told Louis Duffus in the 1960s. "He bowled leg-breaks and off-spinners at about the same medium pace as Bill O'Reilly did for Australia many years later. He could also roll one for a top-spinner that was very difficult to detect. In fact, in 1912 we just never saw it. In addition Syd often opened the bowling and he used to swing the new ball away from the right-handed batsman at more or less the same speed as Eddie Barlow does these days.

"On English wickets he was a real terror but I had a lot of experience batting against googly bowlers and I'd learned to watch a bowler's finger movements as he delivered the ball. This made me quite confident that I would be able to handle Barnes under South African conditions.

"I made no secret of the fact that I was looking forward to batting against him on matting wickets, but I doubt very much if anyone took me seriously. In those days you only had to mention Barnes's name to have batsmen scurrying for cover. Over-emphasis on forward play and poor footwork contributed to many a batsman's downfall against Barnes, but he was nevertheless the finest bowler I ever saw.

"I played Barnes the way I did those magnificent googly bowlers Vogler, Schwartz, Faulkner and White when I first came into first-class cricket. I kept my eyes glued to the ball in his hand as he ran up to the wicket. And just before he delivered it, I would switch my eyes to about a yard above his head to catch any finger movement as the ball left his hand. It was no use picking up the ball after it had left the hand of a bowler like Barnes because you would have no idea what it would do off the pitch.

"Once I knew what sort of delivery it was going to be, it was a case of 'forward to the ball you can meet and back to the ball you can't'. Of course, you have to be quick with your footwork but what I have told you now is the really very simple secret of batting."

In the first Test in Durban in December 1913, South Africa (with seven men making their debut) were all out for 182. Most of the batsmen found Barnes unplayable, but Taylor made 109 – and his wicket was not taken by Barnes. The next best score was Dave Nourse's 19, and only one other batsman got double figures. In the second innings, Barnes got Taylor out for eight runs; he took 10 for 102 in the match, and England won by an innings and 157 runs.

In the second Test at Johannesburg, Barnes took 17 wickets for 159 runs and England won again by an innings. Of the other Tests, the third (by 91 runs) and fifth (by 10 wickets) were also won easily by England.

Only in the fourth match did South Africa stand a chance of victory. They led on the first innings and then declared on 305 for nine in the second (Taylor 93), and the match finished a draw, with England on 154 for five, chasing 313 to win.

Taylor's century in the Durban Test was no fluke. In the Test series, his 10 innings included six good scores: 109, 40, 70, 93, 42 and 87. In the match between Natal and England, the only fixture of the tour in which England were beaten, Taylor scored 91 (out of a team total of 153) and 100 (of 216 for six). "Keeping Barnes's bowling to himself as much as he could," said *Wisden*, "the basis of his play was the straightest of straight bats, nimble footwork, and an almost unfailing judgment of length."

Neville Cardus, writing in *Wisden* in 1955, argued that "the annals of the game provide no proof more convincing than this of supremely great batsmanship; for how possibly could any mortal batsman be subjected to a severer ordeal: Barnes on matting, with wickets falling at the other end all the time? It was perhaps the most skilful of all Test performances by a batsman. HW Taylor must be counted one of the six greatest batsmen of the post-Grace period."

John Arlott wrote that "Taylor was said to be the one batsman in the long career of Sydney Barnes who frustrated him. So well and so consistently did Taylor bat against Barnes that the bowler himself became exasperated to the point of an outburst on the pitch: 'Taylor, Taylor, Taylor all the time!' – and threw the ball on the ground." The English cricketers, said HS Altham, "were unanimous that finer batting than his against Barnes at his best they never hoped to see".

Taylor was educated at Michaelhouse, where he was coached by the Sussex professional George Cox, and his 20-year Test career began in the 1912 Triangular Tournament (England, Australia, South Africa) in England and ended with the tour to Australia of Herby Cameron's team in 1931–32, when Taylor was 42. He played in 10 series, was captain in four, and in 42 Tests made 2936 runs at an average of 40.77. He also played rugby for Natal and the leading English club Blackheath. Like many other cricketers, his career was interrupted by World War I, in which he was awarded the Military Cross for bravery.

In South Africa's first series after the war, in 1921, Warwick Armstrong's Australian side called at South Africa on the way home after whitewashing England. South Africa battled in all three Tests, and Taylor's best scores were 47 and 80 in six innings.

In the 1922–23 season, playing against the MCC in South Africa, Taylor was in outstanding form. In the first Test, in Johannesburg in December 1922, South Africa won by 168 runs. The winning margin was almost the same as Taylor's contribution of 176 in the second innings. In the third Test, in Durban, Taylor made 91 in a total of 368. That match was drawn, and so was the fourth Test, in which Taylor "played a masterly game" in the second innings. He made 101 in South Africa's 247 for four, chasing 326 to win. There was another century for him in the fifth Test – 102 out of 234 in the second innings, with Dave Nourse's 25 the next best score – but England won by 109 runs.

Taylor finished the series with 582 runs at 64.66 and was the highest scorer on either side – and that England side had great batsmen like Andrew Sandham, Phillip Mead and Frank Woolley. Taylor's total was also a Test record in a series for a captain, later overtaken by Donald Bradman in 1936.

When the international rankings system was devised in the 1990s, it was calculated retrospectively that Taylor reached a peak rating of 844 (out of 1 000) after his century in February 1923 in the fifth Test against England. He was the only batsman between 1912 and 1928 who displaced the Englishman Jack Hobbs from the top of the batting rankings.

In 1924 in England, Taylor had a poor tour by any standards. In 11 matches before the first Test, he scored just two fifties in 18 innings. In the first Test at Edgbaston he scored seven, the top score as South Africa, replying to England's 438, were dismissed for 30 in 12.3 overs – the record for the lowest Test total, and the only occasion in Test history that no batsman reached double figures. "Today the South Africans gave us the extremes of batting on a good wicket," wrote the *Daily Telegraph*, "ranging in the space of a few hours from sheer rank bad in their first innings to some splendid hitting in their second as the England bowlers tired." South Africa made 390 all out, to lose by an innings and 18 runs. "It is idle to speculate as to why several men in succession cannot face the music at noon or thereabouts, and then an hour or so later face it with confidence and ease."

Wisden summed up Taylor's tour by saying "it is no injustice to him to say that he fell far below the expectations of his friends. The responsibility of captaining a losing side proved rather too much for him, and in the Test Matches he did not do himself justice. He had not in any way lost his form, but circumstances were against him. Taylor's style is so good and his back play so exceptionally strong that one never while watching him has the least doubt as to his class as a batsman."

Apart from his undoubted ability as a batsman, acknowledged by all his contemporaries, Taylor also gained a reputation for getting his side out of trouble – and often then going on to make a big score. An example of this was his next century, which came in the fourth Test against England in January 1928 at the Wanderers, won by South Africa by four wickets. "By restrained methods he gradually obtained a mastery over the bowling and then hit so freely that he scored 101 out of 170 in two hours and twenty-five minutes. In registering the first 100 made against the visitors during the tour, Taylor, though his innings was not faultless, gave a capital display of driving and leg-hitting."

In the 1929 series in England, Taylor was joined in the national side by the 20-year-old Bruce Mitchell, whom he had coached when Mitchell was a pupil at St John's College in Johannesburg.

Bruce Mitchell was born on Ferreira's Deep mine near Johannesburg. As Louis Duffus wrote, "in the early days of the Rand, the mines were the spiritual home of Transvaal cricket. It was played in the hot glare of shimmering white dumps on a hard soil ground with a matting wicket." Mitchell had his first lessons as a six-year-old from EA "Barberton" Halliwell, a legendary wicketkeeper who had played eight Tests for South Africa in the early 1900s. Halliwell said that Mitchell would "play for SA before he is 20" – a prediction that in the event was only five months out.

And the young Bruce played frequently with his sister, who loved cricket and played for the Wanderers Ladies XI. As a reward for scoring 65 in a ladies' match, she won a bat presented by Jack Hobbs, who was on tour with the MCC in the 1913/14 season. She later gave Bruce the bat, which he treasured: "I was always Jack Hobbs when I went in to bat."

Mitchell's side-on stance and emphasis on back play owed much to Taylor's coaching, and he perfected his stance by practising in his bedroom in front of a mirror. At age 13 he was already playing in the St John's 1st XI, and in his last year he scored 648 runs for an average of 49, and took 67 wickets at 16 runs each.

Picked as a slow bowler for Transvaal against Border in 1926 at the age of 17, Mitchell took 11 wickets for 95 runs. His batting only really started to develop the next season, and soon he was going in at number three for Transvaal. When he was chosen for Nummy Deane's 1929 side to tour England, he was himself not sure if he had been picked as a batsman or a bowler. He began the tour as a number seven batsman, scoring 83 in the opening fixture against Worcestershire. By the first Test at Edgbaston, he was opening the innings.

England made 245 in their first innings at a rate of more than three runs per over; in reply, South Africa batted half as quickly, scoring 250 against a powerful England attack. "What Mitchell accomplished on that occasion," wrote *Wisden*, "might be accorded a special place in the history of Test cricket; he went in with Catterall and England did not see the back of him for seven hours. Although during that time Mitchell scored only 88 runs (in 470 balls), and the remarkable patience and endurance he showed made his innings somewhat featureless, there was no mistaking that he was a first-rate defensive batsman and no mean exponent of the off drive."

Gideon Haigh argued that "Mitchell's debut was more of a challenge than most. In common with almost all the young Springboks, Mitchell played his first big games on matting, and as a result mostly off the back foot. When he went to hook Harold Larwood early, the ball was on him far more quickly than he'd bargained for and dislocated his thumb, deadening his right arm and depriving him of all power. He batted on in pain, with only his top hand coming through like a pendulum – something he had cultivated by hours in front of a long mirror at home. He enjoyed a laugh – a private one – when a spectator asked whether he thought he was a war memorial." Mitchell made 61 in the second innings, but could make only another 102 runs in the series and finished with an average of 31.37.

Taylor, however, did rather better on that 1929 tour. He scored his first Test century outside South Africa in the fifth Test at the Oval. *Wisden* reported: "The start of the South African innings proved truly deplorable, for in 35 minutes before lunch they lost three wickets for 25 runs. Thence forward, however, everything went well for them. Their recovery was entirely due to a great partnership by Taylor and Deane who added 214 in three hours and ten minutes. The batting of both men reached a very high standard and, coming as it did in such circumstances, was easily the best in point of class and skill shown by the South Africans in the whole series of Tests." The stand was a South African record for the fourth wicket until beaten in 2003 by Jacques Kallis and Gary Kirsten. The century gave Taylor a total of 221 runs in the series at an average of 55.25. The tour report in *Wisden* commented that, although he wasn't the dominating personality of previous years, he was still the man England had most to fear.

The next opportunity for Taylor and Mitchell came with the five Tests against the MCC team that toured South Africa in 1930–31.

In the first Test, Mitchell made 72 in the second innings (the top score of the match for either side) and South Africa won the match by 28 runs, with EP Nupen taking 11 for 150. In the second Test at Newlands – played for the first time in South Africa on a turf surface instead of matting – Taylor made 117 in a total of 513 and gave "the most attractive batting display for South Africa". England had to follow on but the four-day Test was too short for South Africa to force a result. There were two other South African centuries in the match: Mitchell (123) shared in an opening stand with Jack Siedle (141) of 260. This remained the first-wicket record for South Africa for more than 70 years, until Graeme Smith and Herschelle Gibbs put on 368 against Pakistan in 2003, also at Newlands.

Taylor top-scored with an unbeaten 64 in the second innings in the third Test and then 72 in the fourth Test; Mitchell made 68 and 74 ("playing far more freely than usual") in the fourth Test and 73 in the fifth. Mitchell topped the batting in the series with 455 runs for an average of 50.55. South Africa won the series 1-0.

Taylor's final series in 1931–32 in Australia was also the only time that South Africa came up against the greatest batsman the world has seen, Donald Bradman – and he was at his best. He scored 806 runs, including two double-centuries and two other centuries. South Africa lost all five Tests, played to a finish as was the practice in Australia in those days.

In the first Test at Brisbane, Australia made 450 on a firm, true pitch. Gideon Haigh tells the story of how Bradman was dropped twice, by Cyril Vincent and Mitchell, on his way to making 226:

"Vincent dropped Bradman, then only 10, at second slip, and commenced a suitable chorus of effing and blinding. 'You should not say things like that, Cyril,' Mitchell said mildly from first slip. 'Not even when you have dropped Don Bradman.' Bradman was on 16 when he snicked another outswinger, this time straight to

Bruce Mitchell: slow but reliable, elegant and absent-minded, he was South Africa's most prolific scorer in Tests until the post-isolation era

Mitchell, who also put him down. Mitchell looked at the ball on the ground, shut his eyes, and said almost inaudibly: 'Jesus Christ.'"

South Africa replied steadily enough with 126 for three wickets by the end of the Saturday's play. Sunday was a rest day, but Monday and Tuesday were both completely rained out and "for the rest of the match the conditions were all against the visitors". Pitches were not covered, and one observer described how "the ball lifts off the wicket as though it were photographed in slow motion, and with it come blobs of wet soil. From the boundary, you wonder sometimes how the batsman is not misled into attempting to push a cloud of mud through the covers." In these conditions, Mitchell batted for 70 minutes without scoring. In the end he was run out for 58, the top score; Taylor was next highest with 41 – they made more than half the team's 170. Taylor top-scored in the second innings with 47, and Mitchell recorded the first of three ducks in his Test career.

South Africa lost the first two Tests by an innings and the third by 169 runs. In the third, Mitchell "made six catches, the one that disposed of Woodfull being described as brilliant. It is not flattery to describe him as a slip fieldsman of the first flight." In the fourth Test, Taylor made 75 and 84, and Mitchell 75 and 95 – the four highest South African scores across two innings – but this was the match in which Bradman made 299 and Australia won by 10 wickets. Australia scored only 153 in the fifth Test, but South Africa were dismissed for 36 and 45, losing by an innings in just one day and 88 minutes.

With his side outclassed, Mitchell topped the batting averages for South Africa, and "earned golden opinions during the tour for his admirable slip fielding".

Taylor retired at the age of 43 after the tour to Australia, after a 42-Test career (batting average 40.77) and 26 years of first-class cricket (41.86). EW Swanton wrote in the 1974 *Wisden* obituary of Taylor: "His method was so sound that he remained a beautiful player when nearer fifty than forty, and it was in this autumn of his career that I met him and played a little with him. He was an inexhaustible cricket talker, and despite his own playing orthodoxy propounded unusual theories. One recalls him holding genial court under the oaks at Newlands, and at Lord's during frequent visits to England. He was a man of much charm and that modesty regarding his own achievements which is so often a virtue of the great. In terms of length and distinction of performance it could be said that no-one ever served South Africa better."

Three full years then passed without Test cricket for South Africa. In the 1935 series in England, Dudley Nourse and Eric Rowan joined Bruce Mitchell in the national side, and together these three would provide the team's batting core until the early 1950s.

Dudley Nourse had the mixed blessing of being the son of a famous cricketing father. Dave Nourse's first-class career spanned 228 matches and 40 years. After coming to South Africa as a 17-year-old with the British army, he played in 45 consecutive Tests between 1902 and 1924.

Dave Nourse displayed little interest in his son's cricket, however. Louis Duffus tells the story of one of those endless back-garden cricket games that boys play. One of his friends in Durban told Dudley he didn't know how to hold the bat, and there was a heated argument. Eventually all the boys agreed that Dudley's father would be asked to settle the matter, and they went into the house. But old Dave Nourse simply said: "Son, I learned to play cricket with a paling of a fence. Now you go and do the same." This rebuttal, wrote Duffus, "must have left a lasting impression in Dudley's mind. If that was how his father felt, he would teach himself. Never again did he ask anyone's advice." (However, he had the rare experience of playing in the same first-class match with his father – they represented Natal and Western Province respectively in the early 1930s.)

Eric Rowan attended Jeppe High School for Boys, one of the great South African cricket nurseries. He was vice-captain of the 1st XI in his final year, when the school magazine noted that he had been "both unlucky and disappointing as a bat, but has recently shown signs of recovering form. A much-improved fielder. Very bad between the wickets. With experience should develop into a fine player, but at present lacks the right temperament." As Rowan's biographer Rick Smith pointed out, "the last was a criticism he would lay to rest as he became one of the game's toughest competitors. Afraid of no one, and able to extract every ounce of ability he possessed, he made himself into one of his country's most dependable batsmen." That temperament would also get him into

© Gallo Images/Getty Images/Bob Thomas

Dudley Nourse: stocky, powerful and aggressive, he scored heavily while also propping up the weak sides of his era

frequent trouble with the cricket authorities, costing him not a few Test caps.

Unlike Dave Nourse, Rowan's father Alf was prepared to give his son advice: "Keep your eye on the ball, and when you hit it, hit it hard." After Eric was bowled first ball in a club game by the great EP Nupen, his father gave him a cuff across the ear and said: "If ever I see you frightened again when you go in to bat, you'll get a good hiding and I'll stop you playing."

Nourse's heavy-scoring record for Natal in the Currie Cup ensured him a place in the 1935 side. In the Tests he managed just one 50, but he averaged 41 from 1681 runs in first-class tour games. He scored a century in each innings against Surrey in May, 148 against Oxford University and an unbeaten 160 against Warwickshire.

Rowan earned his place on tour ("I was pleased just to get in") with 408 runs in the Currie Cup at an average of 51, including 168 against Free State in the final game of the season.

The first Test, in Nottingham, of 1935 was drawn because of rain. The second Test, at Lord's, proved to be one of the great events in South Africa's cricket history, with victory by 157 runs and an innings by Bruce Mitchell that would be seen as the finest of his distinguished career.

South Africa batted first and made a modest 228 (Mitchell 30, Rowan 40, Nourse 3); England replied with 198. Mitchell, a plaster above his eye after being hit in a previous match, and Siedle came out to open the second South African innings, and "there followed the classic batting of the match, with Bruce Mitchell, very strong in back play, watching the ball right on to the bat, and making the off-drive perfectly". He put on 104 with Rowan (44) for the second wicket and 101 with Chud Langton (also 44) for the seventh. When Mitchell had reached 164, made in five and a half hours (CB Fry said he "batted like the schoolmaster of all the bowlers ever born"), captain Herby Wade declared on 278 for seven, setting England a target of 309 in four and three-quarter hours to win.

It was "by no means an impossible task", opined Howard Marshall in the *Daily Telegraph*. "I suggest that it would have been far more fitting for England to go down fighting for victory instead of fizzling tamely out in miserable defensive ineptitude. They chose to fizzle however, and soon after tea were ignominiously routed for 151. We may, perhaps, wonder what manner of devastating blight has fallen on English cricket, but that does not in any degree lessen the South African triumph. They are great-hearted players, dour and skilful and swift on the kill." It was the first Test win ever for South Africa in England.

In the third Test at Leeds, Nourse did not play. Rowan top-scored with 62 in the first innings, and Mitchell with 58 in the second. "Rowan alone played England's bowling at all well," said *Wisden*. "Neat footwork and beautiful off drives featured in his innings of nearly three and a half hours. His dismissal by Hammond – a low catch taken on the slip fieldsman's left side with both hands – was a memorable incident of the match." South Africa were set a target of 340 and finished with 194 for five.

Nourse returned for the fourth Test at Manchester, and made 53 (building on Mitchell's 48 in three hours and 45 minutes, and Rowan's 49) as South Africa crawled to 169 for two in 83 overs, chasing just 271 to win. *Wisden* reflected the general view that the tourists were more concerned with ensuring a draw, so preserving their 1-0 lead in the series, than in winning the game: "Although stubborn methods by the South African players in their second innings were understandable in view of the great keenness of the tourists to win a rubber in England for the first time, much of the true spirit of cricket was missing from the final stage of the match." Mitchell did say that he wanted to play his normal game, but that he "found great difficulty in getting the ball away".

Mitchell triumphed again in the fifth Test at the Oval, making

128 in four hours and 40 minutes. "Never taking the slightest risk, Mitchell remained master of all the bowling brought to bear against him. Far from developing more freedom as his innings progressed, he treated the bowling with unnecessary respect. All the same, he was remarkably sound in style, defence and command of strokes." In the match 1 297 runs were scored and only 22 wickets fell.

So South Africa took the series 1-0. Howard Marshall wrote that "our praise is unqualified, and we salute as pleasant and attractive a team of cricketers as ever came from overseas. Individually and as a team they proved admirably capable of rising to the occasion."

Although they had their moments, the Test averages of Nourse (26.16 from four matches) and Rowan (27.33 from five) were those of beginners still establishing themselves. Rowan did average 44 from nearly 2 000 first-class runs on tour, and made 171 in a partnership of 330 with Mitchell (195) against Surrey.

The 1935 tour of England was a triumph for Mitchell. He scored 1 451 runs at 45.34 to finish second in the tour averages, and took 35 wickets at 19.02 to top the bowling. He headed the Test batting figures with 488 runs at 69.71, making centuries at Lord's and the Oval. He was chosen as one of *Wisden's* Cricketers of the Year in its 1936 edition: "As a batsman he is one of those who strike the eye by grace of style; he plays with a quiet, calm deliberation, makes the most of his five feet 10 inches, in getting well over the ball and in his footwork is superb. He always seems to have plenty of time for his strokes and his off-drive is so beautifully done that for such an essentially steady and defensive player his innings rarely become dull to watch."

The South Africans were judged to have been exhausted by the tour, which consisted of 39 matches spread over nearly five months. They arrived back in South Africa at the end of September 1935, only six weeks before the Australians arrived for a four-month, 16-match tour.

Mitchell was not at his best – in seven matches against the

Eric Rowan: cocky, courageous and controversial, he missed several Tests for non-cricket reasons and was retired too early

tourists (including two for Transvaal), he passed 50 only once. This was the Test series made memorable by Dudley Nourse's magnificent double-century in the second Test over Christmas in Johannesburg.

South Africa did poorly in the first innings of that match, making 157 (Mitchell 8, Rowan 38, Nourse 0) in less than three hours, to which Australia replied with 250. In their second innings, South Africa were 90 for three, still trailing by seven runs and "badly placed", according to *Wisden*, "when Nourse and Mitchell came together. Thanks to these two batsmen who added 129, the score reached 254 for four at the close of the second day and Nourse, receiving consistent help, went on to complete the highest score ever hit in a Test match for South Africa. He often ran in to drive the slow bowlers and seldom has Grimmett suffered such severe treatment." The *Daily Telegraph* reported that Nourse "completely collared the bowling, and delighted the 10,000 crowd. He drove powerfully on each side of the wicket, and his aggression caused even such a wily bowler as Grimmett to lose his accuracy."

Nourse made his 231 in eleven minutes short of five hours (off 298 balls, with 36 fours). In South Africa's total of 491, Mitchell's 45 was the second highest score. Australia needed 399 to win and when a Highveld thunderstorm put an end to the match at 2.45pm on the fourth and final day, Australia had eight wickets in hand and still needed 125. Stan McCabe made an amazing 189 not out in their total of 274 for two.

Australia had won the first Test by nine wickets. Though Nourse (91) and Rowan (49, after his 66 in the first innings) had "thoroughly mastered the bowling" in putting on 118 runs in even time for the fourth wicket in the second innings, the Australians needed only 102 to win.

The last three Tests were won by an innings by Australia, and the essence of their dominance was that the South African batsmen simply couldn't handle the bowling of Clarrie Grimmett and Bill

O'Reilly. In the third Test Grimmett took 10 for 88; in the fourth Test, he took seven wickets at less than six runs each in the second innings; and O'Reilly bowled 21 overs, conceded only 20 runs and took five wickets. In the fifth Test Grimmett took 13 wickets for 173 runs – "his flight and leg-break always worried the home batsmen".

In these circumstances, Mitchell's unbeaten innings of 48 in the fourth Test and 72 in the fifth were seen as admirable, as were Nourse's scores of 44 not out, 50 and 41 after his massive 231. Rowan missed two Tests.

As was normal in those days of travel by ship and tours lasting many months, the next series involving South Africa started two years and nine months after the last Test against the 1935–36 Australians. In fact, in the whole decade of the 1930s, South Africa played in only six series – an average of about five Tests every two years. In between there was competitive domestic cricket in the Currie Cup. However, in those days it was the SA Cricket Union's custom, so strange to the modern observer of cricket, not to hold the Currie Cup in a summer when Australia or England was touring South Africa, on the grounds that a domestic competition would be a distraction. So our leading players were usually lacking match practice when they did get a chance to play Tests at home.

The memory of the 1938–39 series against England is dominated by the Timeless Test, covered in detail at the beginning of this chapter. Percy Chapman's team was the first fully representative one to be sent to South Africa, including some all-time great players like Les Ames, Bill Edrich, Wally Hammond (captain), Len Hutton and Hedley Verity. It was also the first tour of South Africa in which no matches were played on matting.

In the first Test in Johannesburg, Mitchell (having scored 133 for Transvaal against the MCC) and Nourse both made 73 in South Africa's first innings of 390. England set South Africa a winning target of 324 in 165 minutes – "a clearly impossible task", said

Wisden. "Mitchell, concentrating wholeheartedly on keeping up his wicket, made only 48 in the available time." The team crawled to 108 in 51 overs.

In the second Test, South Africa had to follow on after England posted 559, despite Nourse's fine 120 out of a total of 286. In the second innings, Eric Rowan (89 not out) "set to work with Van der Bijl to save their side" and they put on 147 for the third wicket to force a draw.

In Durban in the third Test, England again posted a big first innings (469 for four, Eddie Paynter 243) and again a fine, fighting century by a South African was not enough to rescue his side. In their first innings, "on a wicket far from awkward, South Africa adopted a back-to-the-wall policy which played into the hands of the England bowlers". They collapsed from 60 for none to 103 all out. Mitchell top-scored with 30, and then in the follow-on he made a "splendid" 109, including a partnership of 121 with Rowan (67). "Rowan made sure defence his sheet-anchor, and he succeeded so well in his self-imposed task that he did not hit a boundary during the three-and-a-half hours he defied the England attack." South Africa managed an impressive 353, but still lost by an innings and 13 runs.

The fourth Test in Johannesburg was a rain-ruined draw, after South Africa had made 349 for a first-innings lead of 134. Rowan (85), Mitchell (67) and Nourse (38) were the three leading scorers. Rowan and Mitchell "gave their side the lead in a fine third-wicket stand which realised 116 in under two hours. Mitchell batted faultlessly, with powerful drives and strong hits to leg his chief means of run-getting … Rowan's early watchfulness did not please the spectators. His innings, occupying nearly three and three quarter hours, included only five boundaries."

Mitchell was the leading scorer for his side in the 1938–39 series – 720 runs at 65.45 in all matches against the tourists, including 466 runs at 58.25 in the Tests. Like Nourse and Rowan, his career was then suspended by World War II, which began in September 1939. At that stage Mitchell had played 32 Tests and scored 2 399 runs at an average of 45.26. Nourse had firmly established himself (14, 1 097, 49.86), while Rowan (12, 727, 34.61) had yet to become the controversial character of the late 1940s and early 1950s.

Six months after the England tour ended, war broke out in Europe. Three of the players who appeared in the Timeless Test were killed on active service: the Yorkshire left-arm spinner Hedley Verity died in Italy; Essex fast bowler Ken Farnes was killed in an air crash; and South African bowler Chud Langton died in 1942 from wounds received in battle. Mitchell served with the Transvaal Scottish, Rowan in an armoured car regiment. During Nourse's war service in the Middle East, he was said to have hit nine sixes off nine balls in a match in Alexandria.

The next Test series for South Africa came in 1947, the summer remembered in war-weary England for wonderful sunshine and the prodigious run-scoring of the Middlesex "twins", Denis Compton and Bill Edrich, who scored more than 6 000 runs between them – but also for the visit of Alan Melville's Springboks. "There was all summer in a stroke by Compton," wrote Neville Cardus – and the same might have been said of the elegant Melville, who during this series achieved the rare feat of four Test centuries in consecutive innings.

Rowan was left out, apparently because the selectors wanted to blend youth with experience. But there was also a strong rumour that Melville did not want him in the team. Rowan's form in the Currie Cup in 1946–47 was mixed: he made 256 runs at 32.00 with two fifties. "Disappointed? I was bloody mad," he said years later of his omission.

In the first Test at Nottingham, the South Africans surprised the English by scoring a record 533 in the first innings, founded on a colossal 319-run stand by Melville (189) and Dudley Nourse (149) – the highest in all Tests for the third wicket, and the highest for South Africa for any wicket. England then stumbled to 208 all out, and hopes were high for an innings victory for the tourists.

But "in what was probably the most tantalising recovery ever achieved" against South Africa, according to Louis Duffus, England made 551 in the follow-on (Compton 163), thus setting South Africa a target of 227 in two hours and 20 minutes. They managed to get 166 for one – *Wisden* believed "they made no real attempt at the task" – and the match was drawn. Melville's century in the second innings made him the first South African to score two separate centuries in a Test.

In the second Test, a packed Lord's ground watched England win by 10 wickets. Melville made his fourth consecutive Test century, and the next best scores were Mitchell's 46 and Nourse's 61, in South Africa's first innings of 327. In their follow-on, Mitchell dug in and made 80 in 255 minutes and Nourse scored 58 – again the top two scores after Melville.

There was another 80 for Mitchell in the first innings of the third Test at Manchester, and Nourse made 115 in 147 minutes (144 balls) in the second, "in brilliant defiance of the difficult condition of a drying wicket". Batting was difficult in wintry conditions – a freezing wind "frequently lifted off the bails, and on one occasion reached such velocity that it blew down a sight-screen". Even so, South Africa looked like setting England a decent target or at least making the game safe – but apart from Melville's 59, there was little support for Nourse. He hit 13 fours and two sixes: "despite his daring hitting, he made nothing like a mistake, and hooked, square-cut and drove with tremendous power". His innings was in vain: South Africa's last seven wickets fell for 50 runs within an hour, and England won by seven wickets.

At Leeds in the fourth Test, the veterans again were prominent as South Africa struggled to 175 all out – 104 of them from Mitchell (53) and Nourse (51) – and 184, with Nourse top-scoring on 57 ("another gallant rescue attempt"). England won by ten wickets and so led the series 3-0. The Leeds match, said Louis Duffus, "saw the lowest ebb of the side's fortunes. Thereafter they flowed back towards the high-water mark of the first Test match. Melville determined that the tour should not have a mediocre ending." And so the initiative that South Africa had lost swung back to them dramatically in the final Test at the Oval. This was Bruce Mitchell's match. He was on the field for all but 15 minutes of the four days of play, and scored two centuries.

England made 427 all out. Mitchell made 120, and was eighth out when the score was on 293; South Africa reached 302 all out. England then scored quickly – at 4.22 runs per over, nearly double the rate achieved by both sides in the first two innings – and set the tourists a massive winning target of 451. This time Mitchell was unbeaten – he made 189, thus emulating Melville in scoring two centuries in a Test; he put on 184 for the third wicket with Nourse (97). South Africa scored at three runs per over and came within just 28 runs of winning, but with only three wickets remaining.

Although the match produced an exciting finish, it was felt that South Africa could have been more aggressive and could have won, with "a little more enterprise at different periods earlier in the day", as *Wisden* put it. "The position warranted a spirited effort by each side to achieve success, but batsmen and fieldsmen alike seemed worn out by prolonged exercise in scorching sunshine."

However, Mitchell and Nourse were accustomed to having to take responsibility, as nearly all the other batsmen repeatedly failed around them. Their big partnerships in the series were also an indication of the lack of partnerships from any other two batsmen. Nourse scored faster than Mitchell, but neither could evade the defensive attitude that pervaded South African cricket at the time. The Springboks went into games not expecting to win, prepared to be satisfied with a draw, and hoping not to lose.

In a team that "to some extent was forced to adopt a defensive style of batting," Duffus wrote, "Nourse stood out for his virile aggression and consistent response to big occasions. The sight of his stocky figure walking leisurely out to bat inspired a confidence that was very rarely ill-founded." He made 621 Test runs to head the averages at 69 per innings. Mitchell, with 597 runs in the series at 66.33, became his country's leading overall run-scorer in Tests.

These two men and Melville scored 1787 runs between them in the five Tests, 67 per cent more than the rest of the batsmen combined. What might they have achieved with more support, and with more freedom to play their shots in pursuit of reward rather than avoiding risk? And what difference would Eric Rowan, that other pre-war veteran, have made?

Rowan returned to the side 18 months later when England toured South Africa. The series produced one of the most exciting contests in history, in the first Test in Durban. After four days' play in a match dominated but not ruined by rain and bad light, with only three balls to go, any one of four results was still possible – a win for either side, a draw or a tie.

The match started in steamy conditions on 16 December 1948. South Africa made a meagre 161, Dudley Nourse joint top-scoring with 37, and 219. England made 253 in the first innings, and so had to get 128 to win in two and a quarter hours. "From the moment England went in," recalled EW Swanton, "the situation grew in tenseness to a pitch where all emotion was drained."

Only three England batsmen made more than 20; Denis Compton led the way with a doggedly out-of-character 28 in 68 balls, an innings "worth more than many a double century on turf favourable to batting", said Swanton.

Although they slipped to 70 for six at one stage, England crept ever closer to the target, in conditions where the batsmen could constantly have appealed against the light and the fielders battled with a ball that was slippery from the steady drizzle. But both captains scented victory, as the distant lights of Durban North glittered through the early gloom.

Swanton wrote much of his report of the end of the match in the present tense to convey the drama: "When the last eight-ball over began, eight wickets down with only Wright to come, all results were possible. Off the first ball, Bedser, swinging his bat, gives a nasty high chance to Mitchell at slip from which a single is run. The second is on a length on the leg stump. Gladwin catches it on the rise to send it whistling hard and true just a foot or two over mid-wicket's head, and the ball smacks against the pickets in front of the pavilion. The third ball Gladwin, swinging violently, snicks for one to long leg."

John Arlott was broadcasting the match on radio. Let him take up the story: "England 126 for eight – two to win. That was the third ball. If this goes five balls there'll be no commentator left. And Bedser touching his toes there for mental relaxation. Tuckett wiping the ball on the towel. The hills of North Durban completely hidden by rain which is falling steadily round the commentary box. And Tuckett bowls to Bedser, and Bedser swings, and Dudley Nourse has stopped it, and he's going to try and run him out. And he's hit him but he hasn't run him out. 126 for eight. Tuckett to Bedser from the Umgeni end. Two to win. And he's swiped at it – and it hit him in the stomach and it was passing a foot over the stumps and five thousand people appealed and I don't blame 'em.

"Three balls to go, two runs, two wickets. The last over once started must be finished. Tuckett from the Umgeni end to Alec Bedser. A bumper, edged – out to cover. They're going to run. They'll never make it! ... The fielder missed it, the batsmen daren't take the overthrow. 127 for eight. They didn't dare try the over-throw. I don't think either of them has sufficient nerve or sufficient wind, and I certainly have no wind at all. Two balls to go, one run needed, two wickets left. And the two wickets could go just as easily as the one run could come.

"It's a tie. One to win. And two balls to go. And Lindsay Tuckett's got to bowl, and he's bowling to Gladwin. And it's a bouncer and it's outside the leg stump, and Wade in an attitude of prayer prevents it from being byes. And the next one, they've got to run whatever happens. Tuckett from the Umgeni end to Cliff Gladwin. One run to win and one ball to go. Tuckett to Gladwin. And he's knuckled it, and they're running, and Bedser isn't run out, and they've won off the last ball of the over."

If the Springboks had taken two wickets off the last three balls, they would have won; two wickets off the last two balls, and the match would have been a tie – the first in Test history. If England had failed to score a run off the last ball, the scores would have been level but the result would have been a draw – because England had not been bowled out. (In fact the first tied Test was in Brisbane in 1960 between Australia and the West Indies. The only other tied Test, up to 2015, was between Australia and India in 1986.)

Beyond the drama, there was a strong belief among the players that Nourse had not been aggressive enough. He refused to bring in his fielders to save the single, even though his players had heard the English batsmen agreeing to run whatever happened. "Nourse wanted me to bowl at the wicket," recalled the fast bowler Lindsay Tuckett, "but the ball was wet and slippery, and I lost control of one and the fielder couldn't get it and it went to the boundary. I bowled a short one to Bedser and hit him, but Nourse still told me to bowl at the wicket."

Tuckett also noticed that the batsmen were starting to run and were out of the crease before the bowler had released his delivery. He went to Nourse. "I told him I was going to run this bugger out as he was backing up too far." But Nourse said: "We don't do that sort of thing in Test cricket." In fact, it *had* been done before, when Vinoo Mankad dismissed Bill Brown during the 1947–48 tour by India of Australia.

Eric Rowan was critical of Nourse: "They shouldn't have won. It was poor tactics. We should've brought the field in." Rowan's record suggests that if he had been captain on the day, he would have allowed Tuckett to run out Bedser at the bowler's end – as Rick Smith describes it, "the final delivery thudded into Gladwin's thigh and Bedser was nearly down the other end to meet him making the winning run".

In the second Test over Christmas 1948 in Johannesburg, Hutton, Washbrook and Compton scored centuries as England piled on 608 runs. Mitchell made 86, but South Africa trailed by 293 in the first innings, and defeat seemed inevitable. At the end of the third day, South Africa were on 28 for one with a mountain to climb on the final day – Rowan (17) and Mitchell (7) would resume the innings the next morning.

The Johannesburg Test was due to end on 30 December, to be followed only a day later by the third Test at Newlands on 1 January. The selectors believed they had no option but to announce the side for Newlands at the end of the second day of the current match. They did so, and omitted Rowan, presumably because he had made only seven, 16 and eight in the series so far.

Rowan was furious. Going into the last day at the Wanderers, he was determined to prove the selectors wrong. As was often his practice, he went out to bat with no box or gloves. Mitchell and Nourse were no less intent on saving the match. Mitchell stayed in for nearly three hours and made 40; Nourse took more than three hours on an unbeaten 56. Together with Rowan they batted right through the day, with South Africa losing only one wicket in 91 overs and forcing a comfortable draw as they reached 270 for two.

Rowan himself finished on 156 not out, having batted for ten minutes beyond six hours, and throughout the final day. "He allowed himself no freedom till he had seen South Africa safe from defeat," said *Wisden*. When he reached his century, he made a point of turning to where he knew the selectors were sitting and threw a two-fingered "V-sign" at them. When he was later called to explain himself, he claimed that he had actually been showing the "V-for-victory" sign made famous by Churchill. (*Wisden* did not think it appropriate to record this story, though it admitted austerely that "the irony of the situation was apparent to all – not least to Rowan himself".) A record crowd of 75 000 watched the match.

Of course it was too late to include Rowan in the side for the Newlands game, which was also drawn. Again Mitchell (120) and Nourse (112) led the batting with little support – their partnership of 190 was dominant in South Africa's 356. "Their batsmen seldom departed from the utmost caution," said *Wisden*. "Only Nourse showed real aggressive intent." Mitchell scored his last seven runs in 45 minutes, and batted in all for nearly six hours. England made 308 and 276 for three. The victory target of 229, at a rate of about seven runs an over, was not even attempted by South Africa. England were still hoping to win when they had South Africa three down for 83, but Nourse and Mitchell ensured the draw with a partnership of 49.

Rowan returned for the fourth Test in Johannesburg, and was run out for six. But Nourse again came to the rescue, when his side were in deep trouble at four for two. He made an unbeaten 129 out of 257 for nine. Again South Africa were criticised for not going for victory. Set a target of 376, they made 194 for four. "Through their reluctance to run the risk of defeat by attempting a fourth innings task which required fast scoring," frowned *Wisden*, "South Africa refused a chance of victory which might not have been beyond the scope of men more capable of freedom." It was a fair criticism – there seemed to be no reason why Ken Viljoen and Rowan (justifying his recall with 86 in four hours) took 140 minutes to add just 113 runs in the second innings. But Rowan saw his innings as having been crucial in saving his side from defeat.

In the fifth Test in Port Elizabeth, Rowan was out early again, but Billy Wade (125), Mitchell (99) and Nourse (73) led the way to a score of 379. England made 16 runs more, and then Mitchell (56) and Rowan (37) put on a century opening partnership. This cleared the way for Nourse to declare, setting England a target of

172. They reached it with three wickets to spare, in a finish that was almost as exciting as in the first Test in Durban. When Jack Crapp hit 10 runs off three balls to win the game, there was only a minute remaining. England scored at more than five runs an over, which led to more dark comments about South Africa's lack of enterprise throughout the series. But the first and fifth Tests could have gone either way, and the other three were drawn – so the 2-0 series victory for England did not really reflect the balance between the sides.

Having made 475 runs at 52.77 against England, Mitchell was widely expected to be picked again the following season when the Australians visited South Africa. But he made just 23 runs in two matches against the tourists before the first Test. He was perceived to be vulnerable against the Aussie fast bowlers and was dropped, to general astonishment (Rowan had made 29 runs in the same two matches, but he kept his place).

Mitchell immediately announced his retirement. Although he was by then South Africa's most prolific run-maker, with 3 471 runs at 48.88, he had become notorious for slow scoring. (His strike rate in Test cricket was about 30 runs per 100 balls.) However, as *Wisden* pointed out, "for most of his career the South African batting lacked depth, and he was ever-conscious of his responsibility to lay a sound foundation. Had he played in a powerful batting side, there is no question but that he would have reached even greater heights. Possessor of a full range of strokes, he was seldom in a position to bat with absolute freedom, and he somewhat unfairly gained a reputation as a defensive batsman."

John Arlott said of Mitchell that he was "not an easy man to know", but one "in whose brain there is careful labour ... Mitchell is, by nature, a man who solves problems, who solves them for himself, by himself. There are few less obvious or more interesting men in cricket today." *Wisden* said he "sometimes gave the impression that he would have preferred it had Test matches been played in private before empty stands and without the necessity for force or competition. For Mitchell, cricket was a pleasure preferably consumed in silence and deep contemplation."

He was a poor captain: too quiet on the field, and likely to lose himself in his own intense concentration. The wicketkeeper John Waite told the story of a club match where Mitchell and fellow Old Johannian Russell Endean fielded together silently in the slips, as the batsmen at the crease put on a partnership of 150. "Don't you think it's about time our captain tried a change in the bowling?" Mitchell eventually asked his teammate. "You are the captain," Endean replied.

After Mitchell's retirement, Nourse and Rowan remained of the great trio that had come together in 1935, and they proved that they were still the country's leading batsmen. As a team, though, South Africa were outclassed in the 1949–50 series against Australia, losing two Tests by an innings and two others by eight and five wickets. Their opponents included great players like Ray Lindwall, Keith Miller and Neil Harvey.

Rowan did well in the series. His nine innings included scores of 60 (out of a team total of 137), 67, 143, 55, 32 and 40. His century came in the most interesting match, the third Test in Durban. South Africa made 311: when Rowan went out the score was 264 for four, and he had put on 167 for the third wicket with Nourse, who was captaining the side. Then Australia collapsed to 75 all out, thanks to Hugh Tayfield's off-breaks: he took seven for 23 in 8.4 overs.

Nourse had phoned the weather bureau, which told him that more rain was on the way. This meant the wicket would help the bowlers later in the game, so he didn't enforce the follow-on. In the event, the weather bureau was wrong. South Africa were caught on a wet turning wicket and were also shot out cheaply, for just 99. When Australia batted, the sun came out – and they went on to win by five wickets.

The Australian captain Lindsay Hassett said of Rowan: "He was a good, tough player. He would have made runs in any country. He didn't have a lot of polish technically like Nourse, but he had the ability to concentrate and you had to get him out."

Nourse's record in the series was very similar to Rowan's. Although he began with a duck, in nine innings he had scores of 36, 65, 114, 66, 37 and 55. He made 405 runs at 45.00, while Rowan made 404 at 44.88 – far ahead of any other batsman, and both were over the age of 40.

Both men were chosen for the 1951 tour of England, with Nourse as captain and Rowan vice-captain. This partnership was logical, given their veteran status – but Rowan did not respect Nourse as a captain, and the tension between them was a feature of the tour.

The batting highlight of the tour was undoubtedly the double-century scored by Nourse in the first Test at Nottingham. He came to the wicket with the score at 107 for two, carrying a broken left thumb sustained in a county match at Bristol. He refused to have a pain-killing injection because he thought the numbness would affect his grip; a pin had been inserted, and the swelling made it difficult to put his usual blacksmith-like power in his strokes. While he was at the crease 375 runs were scored, and he finished on 208, made in nine and a quarter hours and in increasing pain. As *Wisden* said, "mere figures cannot convey the magnitude of Nourse's performance".

South Africa made 483 for nine declared, enough for a lead of 64 runs on the first innings. But Nourse withdrew from the match after his marathon knock, and no South African made more than 28 in the second innings, which ended on 121 with Alec Bedser taking six for 37.

Victory for England seemed a formality. They needed 186 runs with nearly a whole day to make them. But Rowan had taken over the captaincy. He set attacking fields from the start and encouraged his bowlers, especially McCarthy, to unsettle the batsmen with bouncers. England could score only 25 runs before lunch. In the afternoon, Athol Rowan and Tufty Mann exploited the rain-affected pitch to end up with nine wickets between them, and England were all out for 114, losing by 71 runs. Nourse publicly commended Rowan for his enterprising captaincy. It was clear that the South Africans were popular visitors: 100 000 people watched the match.

Rowan scored a double-century against Northamptonshire, and the next day he was captaining the tourists against Lancashire at Old Trafford. He and John Waite scored 81 before lunch, provoking some slow hand-clapping. This increased after lunch, and the crowd became noisy. Waite remembered that he stood aside from the crease and then sat down, but "still the handclapping went on, and the next thing I looked over and it looked as if Eric was having a suntan on the beach". Rowan lay flat on his back for several minutes, which antagonised the crowd further. Eventually play resumed and Rowan was soon out for 66. In the pavilion he exchanged hard words with a member of the Lancashire committee, and the incident and its aftermath were soon all over the newspapers. Rowan was nearly sent home as a disciplinary measure, and was forced to issue a written apology.

England won the next two Tests convincingly, by 10 and 9 wickets. In four innings, Nourse made just 72 runs and Rowan 91 – though he did top-score with 57 in the second innings at Manchester.

In the fourth Test at Leeds, it was Rowan's turn to make a double-century. Opening the batting in the first innings of the match, he broke Nourse's record of 231 (set in 1935) with a magnificent 236 in over nine hours. When he was sixth out, the score was 480. "Probably Rowan would have enjoyed indulging in bouts of aggression as much as these would have pleased the spectators," noted *Wisden*, "but carrying so much responsibility, he adhered rigidly to his set purpose of building a big total. His concentration and stamina provoked only the warmest admiration." South Africa totalled 538, but England replied with 505 and the match petered out into a draw – though Rowan looked set for another hundred when the match ended with him on 60 not out in the second innings. He remains the oldest batsman from any country to score a Test double-century.

Only 714 runs were scored in the four innings of the low-scoring fifth Test (average 178 per innings), which ended in three days. Rowan top-scored twice with 55 and 45, and England won by four wickets to take the series 3-1. Nourse failed again, scoring four in each innings. In seven innings after his 208 in the first Test, still suffering the effects from his broken thumb, he made only 93 runs – but he still finished second in the averages. On the tour as a whole, however, he made only 673 runs at an average of 25.88, and it was no surprise that he announced his retirement, 16 years after his debut. He was the first South African batsman to achieve a Test average over 50.

Rowan was the best batsman of the tour by some margin, with 515 Test runs at 57.22 – the highest total and average on both sides. Even though he would be 42 when South Africa undertook its next tour, to Australia at the end of 1951, he was seen as a certainty for selection and many people expected him to be named captain.

But his behaviour in the Lancashire game came back to haunt him. He was not selected. The South African Cricket Association stated that he had violated the terms of his tour agreement, and that he had been "a frequent source of worry to other members of the team and to the management". Thus ended the Test career of perhaps the most colourful and controversial player to represent South Africa, though he remained in touch as a selector and administrator, and played club cricket until well into his 50s.

"Eric really gave his life to Jeppe Old Boys and Transvaal cricket," says Ali. "He was the biggest supporter of Transvaal I have ever known. On one occasion we were playing at Newlands and Eric was managing the side. There was this plump and rather officious general manager of the Western Province Cricket Club, which owns the ground. This man came into the dressing-room for some reason and started laying down the law. Eric just looked at him and said: 'Oh shut up. Boswell's circus is looking for fat clowns like you.'" It took about ten years after that for relations between Transvaal and Western Province to thaw.

Ali also recalls that Rowan used to recommend bowling a yorker – a delivery that is pitched well up and therefore hard to hit in the air – to batsmen in limited-overs games who were slogging or going for a big hit. "Now it's common practice to try to bowl yorkers at the death of an innings, but it was first mentioned by Eric in the 1960s."

"Eric really was a mentor to me," says Ali. "He took me under his wing when I came into provincial cricket at such a young age, and he gave me enormous encouragement and confidence. He had a great saying – when we lost, he always used to say: 'Smile, smile, I feel like crying.' That made a big impression on me – winning was so important, but when you lose you mustn't show how upset you are."

Herby Taylor
Born 5 May 1889
International career: 1912–1932

	M	Inns	NO	Runs	HS	Avg	SR	100	50	Conv
Tests	42	76	4	2 936	176	40.77	50*	7	17	29.16
First-class	206	339	26	13 105	250*	41.86		30	64	31.91

Bruce Mitchell
Born 8 January 1909
International career: 1929–1949

	M	Inns	NO	Runs	HS	Avg	SR	100	50	Conv
Tests	42	80	9	3 471	189*	48.88	31*	8	21	27.58
First-class	173	281	30	11 395	195	45.39		30	55	35.29

Dudley Nourse
Born 12 November 1910
International career: 1935–1951

	M	Inns	NO	Runs	HS	Avg	SR	100	50	Conv
Tests	34	62	7	2 960	231	53.81	42*	9	14	39.13
First-class	175	269	27	12 472	260*	51.53		41	54	43.15

Eric Rowan
Born 20 July 1909
International career: 1935–1951

	M	Inns	NO	Runs	HS	Avg	SR	100	50	Conv
Tests	26	50	5	1 965	236	43.66	34*	3	12	20.00
First-class	157	258	17	11 710	306*	48.58		30	54	35.71

* next to strike rate indicates that full details of balls faced are not available and strike rate is estimated from innings where balls faced or minutes batted are available. No strike rate means insufficient details of innings with balls faced or minutes batted are available.

"Conv" is conversion rate from 50 to 100.

PART TWO

GENIUS
CUT SHORT

2

Graeme Pollock

There were early signs of greatness in the cricket of Graeme Pollock. At the age of nine, playing for Grey Junior School against Union High, he scored his first century and then took all the other team's wickets for 25 runs. At one stage during his innings he hit the ball out of the little school ground and into the adjoining cemetery – and was the first over the wall to retrieve it, so eager was he to continue batting.

He played for the Grey High School 1st XI for four years. When he was 16, he became the youngest player to score a first-class century in the Currie Cup, for Eastern Province against Transvaal B at the Wanderers in January 1961. His innings ended on 102 – after he had been forced to wait overnight with his score on 97. When he was 19 he became the youngest South African to score a double-century (209) in a match in Port Elizabeth against the International Cavaliers.

The South African selectors in those days were conservative, usually demanding that a player prove himself over several seasons before being considered for the Springbok team. In the case of Pollock, his talent and early achievements were impossible to ignore and he was picked at the age of 19 for the 1963–64 tour of Australia.

Going into the first Test in steamy Brisbane in early December 1963, six men were making their debut and the team could muster only 86 caps between them – and nearly half of those were Johnny Waite's (41). In retrospect, we know that some of the names would, with Trevor Goddard, form the nucleus of the great South African side of the later 1960s – Eddie Barlow, Peter and Graeme Pollock, Denis Lindsay, Colin Bland – but at that stage those five had just eight Tests between them. By contrast, the Australians had six men who had played Test cricket in the 1950s, and they boasted a total of 214 caps – an average of 20 per man. It was not just a question of the South Africans being underdogs – they were not given a chance, and there were those who asked whether the tour should have taken place at all.

Graeme Pollock made 25, 16 and 2 in his first three innings in Test cricket. Then, in the third Test in Sydney – where he had earlier hit 120 against New South Wales – he scored his maiden Test century. It was an innings of "fierce strokeplay", said *Wisden*, and his 122 included one six and 19 fours.

In the fourth Test at Adelaide, the South Africans turned their talent and potential into runs and wickets for the first time. The highlight of the match was the country's record stand in Tests at that point, the 341-run third-wicket partnership between Barlow (201) and Pollock (175), described as a "merciless assault" on the bowlers. They made the runs in just four hours and 43 minutes, and South Africa's first-innings total of 595 was also a record in Tests. Barlow himself batted for six and a half hours, and later said that his thrilling partnership with Pollock "definitely established a new attacking approach in South African cricket". *Wisden* noted that Pollock threw his bat at the ball "even more joyously than his partner".

"Threw his bat" ... Graeme always favoured a heavy bat, usually a weight of 2lb 14oz – the average for leading players was 2lb 6oz to 2lb 10oz. Why was this important to him? "The weight was in the bottom of the bat," he recalled in conversation with Ali in 2014. "Duncan Fearnley used to make the bats specially for me. My bat had the thinnest grip that you could have on a bat, so it transferred the weight – the weight was essentially in the bottom of the bat. I liked the feel of what was in my hand, I liked the feeling of control. It was a long handle – they're not making long handle bats like that at the moment. I was basically a front-foot player and if you're not a hooker and a cutter, the weight is basically not a factor."

Ali believes Graeme was one of the first batsmen to place his feet further than one foot apart, although a lot of batsmen in the modern game do this. "I would never get over-technical about batting," said Pollock. "You've got less than half a second to do whatever you want to do at the crease if a guy is bowling quickly. So I decided, as a tall guy, to stand with my legs wider, to make it easier to transfer the weight forward or back quickly. I remember talking to the South African team a few years ago, and Hansie Cronje, when he was captain, asked me, 'I want to get back and across – what do you suggest?' And I said, 'Hansie, why don't you start where you want to end up?' It eliminates hassles – the time factor, and worrying about your head being still, and your balance – everything is right with your legs wider. It makes the transfer of weight much easier."

Such was Graeme's dominance of attacks in his 27-year first-class career that it is hard to imagine him being kept quiet by bowlers, or easily dismissed. But there was a view during the tour to South Africa by Mike Smith's MCC team in 1964–65 that the English spinners Fred Titmus and David Allen had him worked out.

In the first Test in Durban, England won by an innings and 104 runs – enough to win the five-match series, because the rest were drawn. "They batted first, it was bone-dry," recalled Pollock, "and they got 485 for five declared. It was a real turner. They bowled around the wicket and Titmus was the guy who did the damage. He was the closest to the guys that bowl the doosra today. He had a delivery that went straight on, whereas normal off-spinners didn't really do that, they turned the ball. He hit the seam on a regular basis and the ball came back into me. I initially got some bat-pads." Pollock was out for 5 and 0 in Durban, both times to Titmus – bowled, and then caught by Mike Smith.

Titmus got Graeme out again in the second Test for 12 – but then he made 55 in the second innings, followed by 73 in the third Test and an unbeaten 65 in the fourth. Though he was improving steadily, it seemed the critics had a point. In the first four Tests he made 245 runs at 35.00. In those four Tests he was dismissed five times by Allen and Titmus, and averaged 20.20 against them.

However, in the fifth Test in Port Elizabeth it was clear that the initiative had passed from the English spinners to Pollock. He made 137 in the first innings and an unbeaten 77 in the second. His fine batting included many drives past cover and mid-on, and it was not his fault that the match ended in a draw: his fast scoring enabled Goddard to declare at lunch on the last day and set England 246 to win, but bad weather ruled out a result.

Did Graeme consciously try to improve his leg-side play in that series against the MCC? "Yes. Initially I was content to score on the off side and if they bowled leg side, I would score ones and twos, I wasn't looking to hit boundaries. I think when I started opening my feet further apart, my balance was better, I was straighter up. If you're a tall guy, and if you follow the old MCC coaching manual stance, you tend to over-balance – the first movement is towards the off side and you tend to go with it, and you struggle to play on the leg side. I decided that if I didn't have to move, and I was standing straight up, I would be able to sort out the leg-side play." He became known for a prodigious pull shot, and developed his on-drive – "but it was based on better balance".

Pollock became known for fast scoring, an aspect of his play that partly explained his great popularity with the crowds. In his youth, people would come from all over Port Elizabeth to watch him in a club game – and his fellow players remembered how, when he was out, there was the immediate sound of car engines being started as people prepared to leave the ground. This fast scoring was not simply a matter of technique and aggression – it was also the result of a calculated attitude.

© Gallo Images/Die Burger/Pierre Schoeman

Graeme Pollock: a star throughout his career, he always set out to dominate the bowling from the start of his innings

"The Australian Bill Lawry said I was the best player of a bad ball that he had played against. I just had a big thing about bad balls: whenever you got one, you had to do something with it. People tend to think batting is about not getting out. That's a factor, of course – but you have to put the bowlers under pressure, that's the whole thing about batting. If a guy bowls you a half-volley, it has to go for four. If he bowls short, it's four runs. Then the bowler will have a totally different mental approach, knowing that he can't bowl a bad delivery against you. And that's when they start bowling badly. You've got to put the bowlers under pressure.

"If you are scoring 80 runs in a session, that's not bad, in those days it was reasonable – but how many bad balls in a two-hour session are you not scoring off? Maybe there are six, eight or ten. Imagine if you hit just five of those rank bad balls for boundaries – then you're suddenly scoring 100 runs a session. You're not under pressure, it's not a risk shot – they're bad deliveries.

"Nobody used to practise hitting a bad ball in the nets – you'd have the bowling machine, everything technically correct, and you'd think you're playing well. I practised hitting bad balls in the nets. I used to ask them to give me full tosses and long hops. Initially, I did that in the nets, and then I developed the confidence that that's just how you've got to play.

"I always went in with a plan. When I went out to bat, I looked at the field and planned where I would hit the ball for four. If he bowled a full toss, it would be hit through cover – or wide of mid-on. I planned for the bad ball and what I was going to do with it. If I got it, I used to chase it."

Pollock hit seven centuries in his abbreviated international career of 23 Tests, including two double-centuries. When asked which innings meant the most to him, it was not the 209 at Cape Town in January 1967, or the 175 at Adelaide in 1964, or the 274 he scored at Durban in 1970 ("it was a good batting wicket and outfield, and we got a good start as a team"), but the 125 he made in the Nottingham Test in England in 1965.

The conditions were among the toughest he'd encountered, and the South African team was under enormous pressure.

"It wasn't easy to bat in English conditions in 1965," says Graeme. "You had to play pretty well – the ball was swinging and seaming around in all three Tests, and we were playing on uncovered pitches. We were always losing wickets – we went into that series with only one opening batsman. Tiger Lance was opening at one stage, and Denis Lindsay in the third Test. We were down two wickets for next to nothing every time."

At Trent Bridge in the second Test (the first at Lord's was drawn), South Africa batted first and struggled from the start. They were 16 for two wickets, then 80 for five – Barlow, Lance, Lindsay, Bland and Bacher were out for just 39 runs among them. Then Peter van der Merwe joined Pollock and they put on 98 priceless runs together for the sixth wicket – but 88 of them went to Pollock. His 125 was made at not far off a run a ball.

Norman Preston, editor of *Wisden*, judged that "this was one of the finest Test displays of all time. It was divided into two parts. In 70 minutes before lunch, Pollock felt his way tentatively while making 34 and seeing the total to 76 for four. Afterwards he reigned supreme for 70 more minutes while he lashed the bowling for 91 out of 102. For the most part Pollock made his strokes cleanly, and he offered no chance until Cowdrey smartly held him at slip." He had 34 off 54 balls at lunch, and scored 91 off 91 balls after lunch.

Peter Pollock took 10 wickets in the match and South Africa won by 94 runs – enough to give them the series, as the third Test at the Oval was drawn (Graeme was bowled by Titmus for 12 and run out for 34).

The other innings that Graeme selects as special was not a century, but the 90 he made in the second innings at the Wanderers in the 1966–67 series against Australia. This was the match where

South Africa achieved its biggest Test victory in its history – but it started with Australia in complete command. Batting first, South Africa crashed to 41 for five wickets (Pollock made five) and only in that context did their first-innings total of 199 seem respectable. In reply, Australia's openers Bobby Simpson and Bill Lawry put on 118 and Australia reached 204 for one – and then lost nine wickets for 121 runs. South Africa made a record total of 620 all out in their second innings and went on to win by 233 runs.

It was in that second innings that the talent in the Springbok team began to assert itself. Six men got past 50 and Denis Lindsay smashed 182 to add to his 69 in the first innings – "yet the gem of the innings," said *Wisden*, "was Pollock's 90. On this display the young left-hander looked without peer and his timing, placing and wristwork were an object lesson for the purist." His runs were scored in less than two hours off 104 balls, and included 15 fours and two sixes – only 18 of his runs were not from boundaries." (Watching him at the other end during a 91-run partnership was Ali, who had made 63 when he was run out: "I was past umpire Baxter, I was in by a yard and a half. The Aussies conned Baxter, because they appealed before the bails were off!")

Pollock tries to explain the quality of that innings of 90 – "everything happened quickly and felt right" – by referring to a century he made in 1969, playing for an invitation side against Barbados in England. "I got 100 in 52 minutes – I made 50 in 26 minutes and 50 in 26 minutes. They had seven West Indian internationals, including Garry Sobers and Wes Hall. Sometimes you feel just right, and that's how it was with that Wanderers knock in December 1966. I started with a six – I got a full toss from Tom Veivers, I hit it into the scoreboard.

"I say to the young players ... technically, if you are looking at getting a hundred, what do you have to do? You've got to hit about 16 boundaries, which is not a big factor, and with your ones and twos you will get a hundred. If you take advantage of the bad balls that you are going to get over a period of time, then you can do it. When I was making that 90 at the Wanderers, the guys bowled badly to me because I was putting them under pressure. I had some unutterable crap dished out and I took advantage of it."

Like the great West Indian Viv Richards, Pollock's philosophy was to set out to dominate from the first ball – and "the speed of scoring on its own puts the bowlers under pressure". Ali recalls that nearly all Pollock's hundreds were fast, made in two to two and a half hours.

At the Wanderers in December 1966, Pollock was batting in the context of an innings where several batsmen around him were hitting aggressively – Barlow (50), Bacher (63), Bland (32), Lance (70) and Lindsay (182). It was a very different story at Newlands in the second Test of the 1966–67 series. The Australian journalist RS Whitington wrote: "Shakespeare created his heroes and so this day did cricket in the clear-cut figure of young Graeme Pollock. It is against a canvas of disaster that the champion stands out."

Australia batted first on a feather-bed pitch, and took ten hours to make 542, with centuries from Bobby Simpson and Keith Stackpole. In reply, South Africa ended the second day on 56 for three. The next morning they were soon 85 for five – and 457 runs behind. The fifth wicket was that of Denis Lindsay, hero of the first Test at the Wanderers, out for just five runs and literally knocked out by a bouncer from Dave Renneburg. The ball glanced off Lindsay's glove, split the skin on his temple and rebounded to be caught by Renneburg as he followed through. Lindsay went off to hospital for stitches, and South Africa's chance of saving the game now rested entirely on Pollock – who was not fully fit, having injured his thigh.

Whitington wrote of Pollock at this stage of the match, after Lindsay's dismissal: "He is as cool as a cucumber, taking stock of the situation and of the calibre of the bowling. He is deciding what can be done about the situation and how it must be done by a man with a half-wooden leg. He has his captain Peter van der Merwe with him now; David Pithey, whose highest Test score is 19; his brother Peter, with a bruised heel; an injured Richard Dumbrill; and off-spinner Athol McKinnon to help him. To avoid the follow-on, 309 more runs are needed, and 458 more to level the scores. Clearly he must get most of them – and quickly."

The Australians had scored their runs at a rate of just 2.87 per over, but Graeme reached his fifth Test hundred in three and a quarter hours and 181 balls. His double-century was made in five hours and 50 minutes. While he was at the wicket the team's total moved from 12 for two to 343 for nine, and he contributed 209 out of those 331 runs.

The former Australia captain Richie Benaud commented in his report of the day's play: "In its context I do not think Pollock has ever played a greater innings. Nothing seemed to trouble him in his complete dominance of the Australian attack. He is the best modern placer of a ball I know." Despite support from Van der Merwe (50) and Graeme's brother Peter (41), South Africa ended up 39 runs short of saving the follow-on. In their second innings, in a severe anti-climax, Graeme was out for four, bowled after groping forward to a ball from Simpson that, wrote Whitington, "turns in and, wonder of wonders, slips and sneaks through the gap, like some thief in the day, to rob South Africa of its young hope. The whole Australian team run from all points of the compass to grab Bobby who is unable to believe his eyes." Australia went on to win the Test by six wickets, thus squaring the series 1-1.

The dominance of Australia in the early stages of the Wanderers Test and their convincing victory in the Newlands game concealed a gap in class between the sides. Eric Rowan was one of the former international players in the press box, and he argued after the second Test that only Simpson, Bill Lawry and fast bowler Graham McKenzie would get a game for South Africa, whereas for Lindsay Hassett's Australian team of 1949–50, only Dudley Nourse and

Rowan himself would have got in. Rowan's analysis was vindicated in the remaining three Tests, as the initiative moved dramatically towards South Africa.

In the third Test in Durban, Pollock failed in the first innings (two runs) but joined Ali in the second innings in what *Wisden* described as a "brilliant unbroken stand" of 127 in 140 minutes for the third wicket – which took the match to victory for South Africa. Pollock made 67 from 155 balls – unusually slow scoring for him.

In the fourth Test in Johannesburg, South Africa were robbed by rain of a crushing victory. The match was drawn, with Australia eight wickets down in their second innings and still 41 runs short of avoiding an innings defeat. Graeme made 22 in South Africa's only innings.

The sides went to the fifth Test with the series still alive, as South Africa was 2-1 up with one to play. The series was duly won by South Africa in Port Elizabeth, but it was a low-scoring, slow-scoring match and the result was by no means inevitable. The only century of the game was scored by Pollock, and it proved crucial in keeping the winning target for South Africa as low as 176 in the fourth innings.

When he was approaching his century in South Africa's first innings, Graeme cut at a ball from Dave Renneburg, and snicked it low from an inside edge. Wicketkeeper Brian Taber took a spectacular catch, and, as Richie Benaud put it, "Graeme Pollock was out for 93 to Renneburg. He thought so himself ... Pollock took two steps towards the pavilion." But umpire Draper did not raise his finger, and "there was general and genuine consternation among the Australians". Not long after, however, Graeme was bowled by Cowper for 105 – the fourth time his wicket had been taken by Cowper, of the seven times he was dismissed in the series. It was his sixth hundred in Tests, and one especially enjoyed by his home crowd in Port Elizabeth because it was achieved on his 23rd birthday. He also became the first South African to have scored four centuries against Australia.

In the second innings, as South Africa won the match with the loss of just three wickets, Graeme scored an unbeaten 33 and was at the other end when Tiger Lance hit the six that clinched the fifth Test match and the series 3-1. At this stage of his career, Pollock had played 19 Tests and his batting average was 57.96. The general view of his ability was summed up by Whitington: "Heaven knows how many centuries he will add if he plays Test cricket for as long as Donald Bradman did and no war intervenes."

However, the Port Elizabeth Test proved to be Pollock's (and South Africa's) last for three years. He had to be content in that time with batting in the Currie Cup. In the 1967–68 season, his first-class average was 50.27, and in 1968–69 he topped the domestic averages with 1 043 runs at an average of 86.91, including three centuries and five fifties.

In the 1970 series against Australia, Pollock made scores of 49, 50, 274, 52, 87, 1 and 4 – 517 runs at an average of 73.85. But his batting in that series is remembered for the record innings of 274. "His concentration never wavered," said *Wisden*, "and he attacked continuously and with merciless efficiency."

Pollock again draws attention to his methodical and consistent scoring. "My 274 in Durban went meticulously at 80 runs per session. After two sessions on the first day I had 160 not out. At lunch on the second day I had 240 not out, and so on. It was good from ball one – Alan Connolly bowled me some half-volleys and I got three boundaries in the first over, and it just flowed from there. I was hitting the bad ball, not hitting the ball in the air ...

"I was always prepared – there was not an innings in a Test where I was not mentally prepared. I was always asking: what is happening out there in the middle, what is the fielding side try-ing to do? You know, we played so little cricket in those days, if you didn't take advantage of the opportunity to bat, you didn't get another one for a couple of weeks. You had to make runs every time. In the early days I used to have a net before a club game in

Port Elizabeth – have a net at 11 o'clock and club cricket would start at one o'clock. Because I always felt I had to get runs."

Ali remembers that, when Graeme was playing for Transvaal, he would come to the nets with gloves, no pads, have 10 or 15 balls thrown at him, and that would be it for the practice. "If I was playing well in the middle, it was sufficient. All I needed to maintain was my eyesight, my sharpness. The nets are a bad place to bat, the nets are crap. Every guy has a new ball, every guy is bowling off 18 yards. They try and knock your block off. After 20 minutes in the nets you come out and you've lost your confidence. If I was having a good run, I never had a net. If I did have a net, I would have someone throw to me rather than a whole mixed bag of guys bowling, because that does you no good. I might get someone like Ray Jennings to do a short, sharp session, hit me a few catches to get the reflexes going. There were no sight-screens in the nets, too, and a lot of batsmen doing some bowling, so it didn't do any good. The main bowlers often didn't bowl in the nets."

Mark Nicholas, captain of Hampshire and later a leading commentator, recalled that "in 1983, I watched the rebel West Indians play South Africa in a one-day game in Port Elizabeth. Barry Richards made a hundred but Graeme Pollock stole the headlines with a vignette of startling bravura. Hit in the head by Sylvester Clarke, he returned to the wicket an hour or so later, well stitched above the eyebrow, to face the remaining five balls of another Clarke over. Needless to say, Clarke went at him hard. Pollock hit all five balls for four or six." Graeme made an unbeaten 66 that day.

Graeme played his last first-class match in March 1987 at the age of 43, at the Wanderers in the Currie Cup final against Western Province. When he came to the wicket in the second innings with Transvaal's score at 31 for two (he had made four in the first innings), everyone knew it was his last innings, and the crowd's applause went on for several minutes. On the scoreboard, instead of the number four position being filled by "POLLOCK" – as it had been in nearly all the 262 first-class matches he had played for any side since his debut in 1960 – the spectators roared when they saw that, between the names of Mandy Yachad and Ray Jennings, the scoreboard operators had simply placed the word "MAESTRO". Graeme then delighted the crowd with a flawless, flowing 63 not out. It was appropriate that he was unbeaten in his last innings – seldom in his career had a bowling attack been able to contain him.

In the last of Graeme's 27 first-class seasons, the statistics show that he was not in decline, even at the age of 43. He topped the South African batting averages in 1986–87 with 456 runs at 65.14, including two hundreds and three fifties.

Who was the best fast bowler he faced? "I would say Dennis Lillee. Sylvester Clarke would come pretty close. Lillee was quick and he was aggressive. What you need to bowl to be successful is to bowl outside the off stump, going away from the batsman – like Dale Steyn is doing, and Richard Hadlee used to do – off stump and outside, he's niggling either way.

"I didn't play against him, but the guys probably rate Wasim Akram as one of the greatest. Jimmy Cook played county cricket for five years – he said Wasim was way ahead of the rest – he was quick and he did everything." This is a view backed in conversation with Ali by Jacques Kallis and Brian Lara.

"Sylvester Clarke was the most vicious bowler I came across," says Pollock. "He was vicious, he was lethal. Whether he threw or not was a contentious issue. If you hit a guy like that square of the wicket with a short delivery, rest assured that the next one would be a bouncer and sometimes the ball went on over the 'keeper's head."

When asked about the best spinner in his experience, Pollock mentions Derek Underwood, but emphasises the Australian "mystery spinner" Johnny Gleeson, who attracted a lot of attention before the 1970 series in South Africa. Ali admits that he never had a clue what Gleeson was bowling. Graeme says the bowler "was under-rated. We got the better of him – but in those days a lot of guys would play him with the pad and you weren't given out. But any bowler with variation can cause problems, and there was a lot of uncertainty with him – if you're not sure what the guy is trying to do, you have to watch the ball like hell. And that affects you, because you're worrying about what he's trying to do, and you're not giving the same concentration to your batting.

"There weren't great spinners around in those days. I played against Richie Benaud in 1963, at the end of his career. Denys Hobson of Western Province was a good bowler, but specifically only in Cape Town, he bowled well there. Bowling into the south-easter, he was a big factor – but now of course there's no south-easter at Newlands because of the new stands they built. Spinners don't even feature in Cape Town any more ... the dip that they used to get was a big factor.

"People ask if the bowlers are quicker today. I point out that the no-ball rule was different in the old days. The bowler's front foot would land a yard in front of the popping crease, so they were bowling a yard closer. I don't think the bowlers were quicker then. As a left-hander you always wanted to be batting first – because of the bowler's footmarks from the second day onwards, where they were allowed to run onto the wicket." (The no-ball law was changed in 1969.)

"Probably the fastest bowler I saw was Jeff Thomson. They say Frank Tyson was the fastest in the 50s, Wes Hall in the 60s, Thomson in the 70s – and then there was Harold Larwood in the 30s."

Who was the best batsman he came across? "Barry Richards and Garry Sobers were the best I've played with. Technically, Barry was as sound a player as you could get – everything was right. Garry Sobers was brilliant. He used to smash them – stand in this upright position and hit the ball straight back past the bowler, off the back foot." Pollock had the opportunity to watch Sobers up close when they shared a sparkling fifth-wicket partnership of 165 for the Rest of the World against England at the Oval in 1970 (Pollock made 114, Sobers 79).

This is how the great English writer and broadcaster John Arlott summed up Graeme Pollock:

"Tall, wide-shouldered and relaxed, his easy timing invests his strokes with considerable power. He has always blended style and an attacking bent with striking deliveries which would force the majority of batsmen on to the defensive ... He established himself as a world-class batsman at an early age. The memory remains of him leaning into the ball and with an almost lazy, long swing of the bat, striking it quite classically, and with splendid force through some skilfully identified gap in the off-side field."

Graeme Pollock
Born 27 February 1944
International career: 1963–1970

	M	Inns	NO	Runs	HS	Avg	SR	100	50	Conv
Tests	23	41	4	2256	274	60.97	56*	7	11	38.88
First-class	262	437	54	20940	274	54.67		64	99	39.26
List A	119	113	20	4788	222*	51.48		13	25	34.21

3

Barry Richards

S ir Donald Bradman, the greatest batsman of all, picked Barry Richards (with Sir Jack Hobbs) as one of the two best opening batsmen he had seen, and chose him for his all-time best XI. Not all experts agree with that selection, but none has disagreed that Richards was one of the truly great batsmen – even though he played only four Tests before South Africa was excluded from Test cricket for 22 years.

John Arlott wrote that "no one who ever watched Barry Richards bat could conceivably doubt his ability. He picked up the line of the ball early, had a wide range of strokes and, when he was in the mood, could toy with the best bowling. He will be remembered as one of the most brilliant players of bowling of modern times."

Colin Cowdrey, himself one of England's leading batsmen and a shrewd judge of ability, was emphatic: "Barry Richards is a great batsman. There is no doubt about that. He is one of the five best batsmen I have ever seen, and the disappointment is that he has been denied an international stage on which to exhibit his talents and demonstrate his power in the record book. Tall and upright, sturdy yet without an ounce of surplus weight, he is very powerful. Blessed with a calm, quite unshakeable temperament, he has a perfect technique which stems from an ability to stand as still as a rock and play the ball better than anyone else I remember. He appears not to move at all, yet his feet twinkle. He makes batting look so easy that when he comes to fail he can give the impression that he has not been trying. This would be quite unfair and a false assumption. No one could be as good as Barry Richards without a deep sense of professional pride."

Richards's grandfather was an early influence. "I was sporting my primary school cap for the first time. When I passed 50 the captain declared, and I duly rushed off to Grandpa, exuding self-satisfaction and expecting nothing but the most lavish praise. Instead I received the biggest telling-off I had ever experienced. He sailed straight into me – for rudeness in not raising my bat or touching my cap to acknowledge the applause of the handful of onlookers. Of course I burst into floods of tears, but the point was made."

Richards grew up in Durban, where he took advantage of the warm climate by surfing and swimming – as a teenager he gained peak fitness by swimming at the large beachfront pool, eventually achieving a routine distance of 3 000 yards a day. He played rugby and squash, but his first interest was always cricket. His early practice method was unknowingly similar to that of Don Bradman in his youth: "When there was no one else around, I would practise for hours on my own, hurling a ball against a wall and batting against the rebound. My 'net' was our garage, my 'bat' was just 12 inches long. This must have been extremely good conditioning for the eye and the reflexes. I used a golf ball, which when I threw it at the wall really used to fly at me on the bounce. It didn't pay to miss, because behind me was the open end of the garage. When I did miss, the golf ball went many a mile and I had to traipse after it."

His cricketing role model was the flamboyant Natal Springbok Roy McLean, as famous for his centuries as his ducks – "I was one of the kids who used to yell out in anticipation when he walked out to bat – what a favourite he was, the South African Denis Compton, all charisma and flowing shots."

At Durban High School he progressed rapidly to the 1st XI and schools provincial selection. Among his contemporaries were Mike Procter and Lee Irvine. In 1963 he was chosen to captain the pioneering South African Schools tour to England. In 1965 he and Procter spent a season in Bristol playing for the Gloucestershire 2nd XI. "Both of us approached our cricket with a dedication that I'm sure the Gloucestershire players saw as naïve," remembered Richards. "Even when there were no matches, we went to the nets every day, practising harder than any of the other lads. We were never discouraged by the economic necessities of a county club which cut off the hot water supply when the first team played away and only the second team were using the nets. More than any experience on the field, I vividly recall the agony of those cold showers after a long work-out on a freezing May morning in Bristol."

The two youngsters did play one game for the Gloucestershire 1st XI, against Peter van der Merwe's South African tourists. The Springboks started well and had the county side four wickets down for 62. Then Richards (59) and Procter (69) came together and put on 116 for the fifth wicket. "Who are these young upstarts from South Africa," Ali remembers asking. "Are they trying to show us up?" This tour match has little other historical interest – the last two days were entirely rained out – except for the curious fact that both Procter and Richards were out to the part-time spin of Graeme Pollock. But it was the beginning of a stellar career for both young Natalians. Procter remained with Gloucestershire, and Richards was to play his county cricket for Hampshire, starting in 1968 when counties were allowed for the first time to employ overseas professionals.

At Hampshire Richards opened at first with the West Indian Roy Marshall, and then a famous partnership was born when another West Indian, Gordon Greenidge, joined the county. He was deemed to be English, and the county's attack was strengthened with yet another West Indian, Andy Roberts. As an opening partnership, Richards and Greenidge complemented each other: artistry and finesse on the one hand, and destructive, explosive power on the other. But Greenidge admitted that "it was not unusual for me to be in single figures as applause rang around the ground for Barry's fifty".

The irony of a black West Indian and a white South African forming such a close and effective partnership was often noted. Occasionally Greenidge and Roberts would leave the county circuit to join the West Indies on tour, and Richards says he often thought that he should be doing the same – and he thought privately that he was a better batsman than Greenidge.

Many believed that Richards should have been capped for South Africa in the 1966–67 season, against Bobby Simpson's Australians. He had certainly done enough in the Currie Cup to earn selection – he finished the season with 553 runs at an average of over 50, with a century and five 50s – and in six innings for Natal and invitation teams against the tourists, he averaged 77.

However, his selection was apparently blocked because of an off-the-field incident that was hushed up at the time: he kicked a pot-plant into a hotel swimming pool in East London after he and a group of players had failed to gain entry to a nightclub, and the selectors got to hear of the incident. No other reason has been advanced for his omission from the Springbok side for the first Test at the Wanderers. Eventually he was selected at 12th man in the final Test, when "my one contact with the ball ended with a wild throw over the wicketkeeper's head. For the rest it was the usual chores, especially forging some of the other players' signatures on the numerous bats that had to be autographed." The punishment may have been unduly harsh, but Richards accepted that "it was entirely of my own making. I then leaned heavily on my father's philosophy that you have to look after yourself in a tough world, and I became more determined to reach my goals."

The main goal, of course, was to play Test cricket for South Africa. But the 1968–69 tour to South Africa was cancelled because of the "D'Oliveira Affair", and Richards, like so many other talented batsmen of that generation, had to be content with domestic cricket – and in the case of South Africa's Currie Cup, domestic cricket was highly competitive.

Ali remembers a Currie Cup game between Transvaal and Natal at the Wanderers in the late 1960s. "Barry was batting, had about 32, I was fielding at mid-off and Don Mackay-Coghill was bowling. After Cogs' third ball I stopped the game. I called Cogs in and told him to bowl on Barry's legs to a packed leg-side field. Barry looked at me and laughed. The next ball, he flicked Cogs into Willie Kerr's hands at leg-gully and he was out.

"When we went round the country on our coastal tour, we told the Eastern Province and Western Province players that it was quite simple to get Barry out – bowl on his legs, packed leg-side field and you've got him. When we went down to Kingsmead for the return match against Natal, Cogs was given the new ball as usual. We wanted to try exactly the same trick and I asked Cogs to bowl accordingly. Running up for his first delivery, he suddenly stopped. 'What's the problem?' I said. 'Look where Barry is standing,' said Cogs – and he was a foot outside the leg stump. So I told Cogs to bowl, and he had no option but to bowl at the stumps that were seemingly wide open. And Barry got a big hundred."

The only opportunity Richards had to play Test cricket was against Bill Lawry's Australian side in early 1970. By this time he was regarded as an automatic selection. He started quietly, with 29 and 32 in the first Test at Newlands.

Richards was the first South African player to work out the bowling of Australia's "mystery spinner" Johnny Gleeson, who was able to deliver off-breaks and leg-breaks on a good length, with no obvious change in his action. The media built up Gleeson's reputation. Ali remembers that "whenever one of our Test batsmen came in during the Aussies' matches against the provincial teams on that tour, and Gleeson was bowling, he was immediately taken off. We never got a chance to see him before the series."

In the first Test, says Ali, "Trevor Goddard got out, and I came in, and immediately Gleeson was brought on from the Wynberg end. For the first two overs he made me look like a clown. When I thought it was the off-break, it was the leg-break; when I was sure it was the leg-break, it was the off-break. Eventually I made a decision – I had to get after him. I put my foot down the wicket and whatever he bowled, I hoicked him over mid-wicket, and I somehow managed to get to 57.

"That night we had a team meeting, and Barry told us how to play him. He said if we could see a lot of fingers on top of the ball, it was the leg-break. If we could only see the thumb and one finger, it was the off-break. He took one look at him and worked him out, and for the rest of the series he ran down the wicket to Gleeson. The rest of us were still a bit wary – even Graeme Pollock played him from the crease – but Barry went after him." In the event Gleeson was unable to prevent a convincing South African victory by 170 runs. "But in that series Gleeson got 19 wickets in four Tests, and there were a lot of dropped catches. He continued to worry most of us, but he never got Barry out once."

The great batting potential of Barry Richards finally exploded into life at Kingsmead in the second Test. After Ali won the toss and chose to bat first, Richards raced to 94 not out at lunch. The total was 126 for two: Trevor Goddard had gone out for 17 and Ali for nine. Ali had run down the wicket to jab the ball to mid-wicket for a single, to give Richards the strike so that he could get his century before the break. Instead Ali was bowled round his legs by Alan Connolly.

Only three men had ever scored a hundred before lunch on the first morning of a Test match: Victor Trumper, Donald Bradman and Charley Macartney. "In retrospect," Richards wrote later, "if I had known I would not play again after that series, I think I would have chased the extra runs." The Australian Ian Chappell recalled that "it was Barry's home ground, so the entire stadium was buzzing with the name Richards. He could have very well

© EMPICS/TOPFOTO/INPRA

Barry Richards: a deep sense of professional pride – and a deep frustration that circumstances prevented him from achieving more

got his hundred before lunch, except Bill Lawry undid his boot-laces and did them up again and wasted a little bit of time."

Richards remembered that "it was one of those days when you were just playing well. I always felt we should be attacking up front and that's what I did. It was just one of those days when, from the first delivery every ball hit the middle of the bat, and with the fast outfield every shot that beat a fielder went for four." His maiden Test century was scored at a strike rate of over 85, and after lunch he and Graeme Pollock put on an exhilarating stand of 103 runs in an hour for the third wicket. Ali has described this as "batting you will never see the likes of again. It was like Barry and Graeme were trying to outdo each other." Richards agreed: "I'm sure my innings spurred him to greater heights."

Richards was out for 140, after "my adrenalin ran away with me. I should have set myself for 200, but I tried to whack every ball. Eventually I missed a slog at Eric Freeman and was bowled. Undoubtedly the best stroke I played came off Gleeson. I ran down the wicket and struck him straight for six." South Africa kept piling on the runs, but Ali refused to declare: "I just thought of how in the past South African teams always got clobbered by Australia and I saw an opportunity to pay them back in some way." The innings closed at a record 622 for nine declared, more than enough to give South Africa an innings victory.

In the third Test Richards made 65, virtually at a run a ball, and 35 as South Africa won by 307 runs. In the fourth Test he con-tributed 81 in an opening partnership of 157 with Eddie Barlow. "When South Africa batted a second time, good bowling and tight field setting forced the opening batsmen to fight for every run," wrote *Wisden*. "Richards again played the dominant part and after Barlow's dismissal ran amok and punished all the bowlers." Richards made 126, his second and last Test century, and South Africa com-pleted another crushing victory over Australia by 327 runs, sealing a 4-0 series win.

"I felt both stimulated and exhausted at the end of the series. Such a flamboyant victory only sweetened the taste for the Test arena," wrote Richards – but none of the members of that great side would play Test cricket for South Africa again. The 1970 tour of England was cancelled, and so was the scheduled 1971–72 visit to Australia.

Richards has a Test batting average of 72.57 in seven innings. The bare statistics tell us that in 18 years of first-class cricket, mainly with Natal and Hampshire, he scored more than 28 000 runs at an average of 54.70 – comparable with Graeme Pollock (54.67), Len Hutton (55.51) and Garry Sobers (54.87) – which places him at 24th on the all-time batting list from all countries. He scored more than 1 000 runs in a South African season five times, more than anyone else. He made 80 first-class centuries, and there is a widespread view that if he had not become bored, he would have scored many more, converting 70s and 80s into big hundreds. Even so, his ratio of hundreds to innings played is 13 per cent, just behind Pollock and Geoff Boycott (14 per cent) and Len Hutton and Walter Hammond (16 per cent).

Nine times he scored a hundred between the start of play and the lunch interval. Three times he carried his bat through a completed innings in first-class cricket, including an unbeaten 225 out of his side's total of 344, for Hampshire against Nottinghamshire in 1974.

After the 1970 Test series, however, Richards became increasingly disillusioned – and he was the most vocally bitter of all the white players whose Test careers were shortened or prevented by isolation. He was like a violinist of genius who was not allowed to play his instrument. His understanding of the fact that many others – especially generations of black players – were more disadvantaged than he was by apartheid does not seem to have reduced his frustration.

In his autobiography, *The Barry Richards Story*, published in

1978, he was unusually candid: "In 1967 no young man could have loved cricket more than BA Richards; ten years later there could be no more disenchanted player in the first-class game, with only the hope of a pirate circus to breathe life into the dying enthusiasm." He had "no challenge beyond that of scoring enough runs to justify the contracts I had signed. Without international cricket, all I had left were personal targets: the most runs in a Currie Cup series, to top the Hampshire averages, and so on. For some time I did burn a candle for a hundred hundreds, but even that died when I realised it only meant an entry on another page in *Wisden*. In the end this inability to cope with targets had become a weakness.

"I suppose it is just the dreadful feeling that for seven years I have been marking time. Even if a miracle happened and South Africa was accepted back into the fold tomorrow, I would hardly be ready for a return. Over the years my fitness has gradually declined, so that I would need six months to get back into shape."

Robin Jackman, the former England fast bowler who played often against Richards on the county circuit, dismissed him more often than anyone else in first-class cricket – 16 times. Jackman has said of Richards that "when you're that talented, you want the world to see it, not a few guys watching at Southampton".

The way Richards achieved his personal highest score, a triple-century, offered a glimpse of what might have been. In the 1970–71 season, instead of playing yet another Currie Cup season for Natal, he was engaged by South Australia. In that state's match against Western Australia, he made 325 runs in a day against a Test-class attack that included a young Dennis Lillee, Graham McKenzie and Tony Lock; and went on to finish on 356 the next day (in 381 balls, with 48 fours).

"I realised during the practice nets before the match what a bouncy track it was," recalled Richards. "It was very shiny and your studs wouldn't go in. There was plenty of pace, and I had never experienced as much bounce as that before. I had no thigh pads, and used socks for protection, and even the gloves I wore during that game were very cheap ones. But I never thought about being hit. My mind was totally focused on using the bat to hit the ball."

Tony Mann was the leg-spinner for Western Australia: "I was the cover fielder and had to run like hell all day. He didn't hit hard but he played beautifully. It was always amazing to watch Barry bat. He placed the ball magnificently – minimal footwork, brilliant eye, very strong wrists – just caressed the ball to the boundary ropes; no big hitting at all. It was his trademark, to find the gaps. Basically he was punching the ball off the back foot. If there was a wagon-wheel, you'd find the lines all around."

Richards missed the first ball he faced, and wicketkeeper Rodney Marsh remembered thinking, "Hello, this fellow's not as good as they're all saying he is. And I said so to John Inverarity at slip. Barry didn't play and miss again for the next 356 runs – in fact, there were only a few occasions when he even missed the middle of the bat. There were very few times I took the ball behind the stumps, because Barry hit almost everything he received, most of them with great force that emanated from superb timing."

Ashley Mallett wrote that "Richards was on 317 when Lillee bowled the last over of the day. The second ball was flayed over cover – one bounce to the fence. The final delivery was a short-pitched ball that rose to above chest height. Most mortals would have done well to fend it to the ground, but Richards went right back on his stumps and somehow swatted the ball over mid-on, one bounce into the crowd."

Marsh's remark at the start of the first day and Inverarity's response have gone down in cricket legend. Richards's version is that "when Lillee bowled the last ball of the day, I simply walked down the wicket, drove the ball back past him to the sight-screen for four, and without breaking stride continued towards the pavilion: 325 not out. Inverarity turned to Marsh, with remarkably quick recall, and commented cryptically: 'I suppose he *can* play a bit.'"

"Recalling that innings now is like a dream," Richards wrote in his autobiography. "Somehow I managed to sustain for a complete day the sort of form that only materialises in short, glorious moments. Conditions, of course, could not have been better, and I think the quality of their attack helped me to maintain a higher level of concentration."

In that Sheffield Shield season for South Australia, Richards averaged 109.86 and scored a century against each of the opposing states – the first and still the only man since Don Bradman to achieve that.

Richards continued playing for Hampshire and Natal, but the closest he came to testing himself in the international arena was in Kerry Packer's World Series Cricket (WSC) in the late 1970s. Packer owned a major Australian television network. Frustrated by the cosy arrangement between the Australian cricket authorities and ABC, the state broadcaster, he was determined to set up a rival organisation so that he could broadcast major cricket. He also believed the commercial potential of the game had not been exploited.

It is hard, more than three decades later, to imagine how little money international cricketers were earning before Packer shook up the game. In 1975 Australian players were paid $400 a Test. The administrators were unsympathetic: "If you don't like the pay and conditions, there are thousands of others waiting to take your place," was one comment. Packer played on this discontent as he worked to set up his rival WSC organisation. He also saw the commercial possibilities of the limited-overs format, which had been launched officially only in 1972, and he was thinking of a 20-over-a-side format 25 years before it happened. It was also Packer's idea to play games in coloured clothing under floodlights – aspects that are now taken for granted, but were highly controversial at the time.

WSC consisted of an Australian XI, a West Indies XI and a World XI, which included several South Africans who were hungry for top cricket after seven years in the cold. These teams played a series of "Super Tests" and limited-overs games. In eight innings Richards made two centuries and two fifties and averaged almost 80 – the highest of all the star batsmen taking part.

In the second Super Test, Richards shared an opening partnership of 234 with his Hampshire colleague Gordon Greenidge. Then Richards added 135 with Viv Richards and the World XI were 433 for one at the close of the first day. Richards finished on 207.

"In the next season," reported Cricinfo, "there was another Richards special, this time in the final of the World Series Super Test. In a tense, low-scoring game, where neither team had scored more than 219, the WSC World XI needed to score 224 in the fourth innings. Richards stamped his presence on the chase with an outstanding unbeaten 101; the next highest score from one of his teammates in either innings was 44. At 84 for four the Australians had a slight edge, but Richards took on Dennis Lillee and Gary Gilmour and ultimately led his team to a five-wicket win."

Richards describes WSC as the "hardest, toughest event I experienced". He was then 34 years old, but in five "Tests" he scored 554 runs against the leading bowlers from the two leading cricket countries in the world at that time, Australia and the West Indies.

Another highlight was a match between Hampshire and MCC, captained by Tony Lewis, at Lord's in April 1974. When Richards was out, the score was 249 for six; he had made 189 and the next five batsmen made 32 between them. He regarded this innings as the equal of his triple-century in Perth. In another context, he was especially proud of the innings he played in his second match for Hampshire in 1968, against Yorkshire at Harrogate. It was an uncovered pitch, and the Yorkshire attack included Fred Trueman, Don Wilson, Brian Close and Ray Illingworth. Richards made 70 out of a team total of 120 – "technically my best innings in extremely difficult conditions".

Richards says the best fast bowler he faced was Michael Holding in the WSC years, but Western Province's Garth le Roux "was as quick as anybody in that tournament". The best spinners he faced were Derek Underwood on uncovered wickets, and Bishen Bedi for his guile and flight.

Robin Jackman of Surrey took Richards's wicket more often than any other bowler in county cricket. In South Africa, the Transvaal fast-medium bowler Don Mackay-Coghill got him out eight times in 16 first-class matches – and would greet him every time he came to the wicket with the tally at that point: "Barry … seven times!" And Richards would laugh and ask: "But how many runs have I scored off you in those seven innings?"

Richards did not have the chance to play international ODIs, but in domestic matches he hit 8 506 runs with 16 centuries and 50 half-centuries. His talent and temperament were ideally suited to the shorter game. John Arlott wrote that "especially in limited-overs matches he would perpetrate strokes of an unparalleled extravagance. He would for instance, step away to leg to an off-break pitched on, or outside, the leg stump, and play it against the spin for four through the covers; or pick up a left-arm breakaway from outside the off-stump and, with something near laughing contempt, simply whack it over mid-wicket for six."

After he retired from playing cricket in 1983, Richards spent a considerable time as a successful administrator – a record that is not acknowledged in South Africa. He was CEO of Queensland cricket for 10 years; during that time he oversaw the redevelopment of the Gabba ground to a capacity of 34 000, and appointed the influential coach John Buchanan. He described this as his best time in cricket off the field. For two years he was also director of Natal cricket: "I can remember working with him in KwaMashu in 1987," says Ali, "and I was impressed with his abilities as an administrator."

Richards feels he has not been acknowledged by South Africans for his immense talent and remarkable achievements. Ali concurs with that viewpoint.

Barry Richards
Born 21 July 1945
International career: 1970

	M	Inns	NO	Runs	HS	Avg	SR	100	50	Conv
Tests	4	7	0	508	140	72.57	59	2	2	50.00
First-class	339	576	58	28336	356	54.70		80	151	34.63
List A	233	229	17	8506	155*	40.12		16	50	24.24

4

Colin Bland

When he was at his peak in the mid-1960s, Colin Bland was widely regarded as the greatest fielder in the history of the game. Fifty years later, he arguably retains that status, despite the general improvement in fielding. Bob Woolmer believed that Bland had "never been equalled in his ability to pick up the ball on the run and get it in flat, hard and accurately". There had been other outstanding fielders before Bland – Jack Hobbs and Donald Bradman, for instance, were feared for their speed and accuracy while patrolling the covers. Clive Lloyd and Peter Kirsten achieved a similar reputation in the 1970s. In the modern era, Jonty Rhodes invented the "slide", achieved some spectacular catches and run-outs, and was a sensation at the 1992 World Cup; and AB de Villiers has made some astonishingly acrobatic dismissals.

But nobody before or since Colin Bland has attracted such interest for his fielding alone, or has dedicated so many hours of lonely practice to this skill. He was the first cricketer to be the hero of small boys purely for his ability to cut off seemingly certain boundaries, return the ball to the wicket as if from a rifle, and throw down the stumps to make spectacular run-outs. Ali likens Bland's fielding to "poetry in motion", and is of the view that "his accuracy in throwing the ball over the stumps was unequalled".

During the 1965 tour of England, such was the interest in Bland's fielding that he was persuaded to put on a special one-man exhibition at Canterbury in Kent. Several thousand people came to watch, and he did not disappoint them, frequently hitting a single stump from 30 to 40 metres out – the work, wrote the English journalist Michael Melford, "of an athlete who had brought the art of picking-up and throwing to a new level". The crowd, wrote Trevor Bisseker, "were fascinated by his wonderful demonstration of stretching while at full pace, picking up the ball and throwing down a single stump while still on the move".

Bland's reputation, continued Bisseker, meant that in all cricket "he saved many runs through his speed and the incredible accuracy of his throwing. His mere presence caused batsmen to turn down apparently safe runs for fear that he would perform a miracle." It was said that his ability to deter batsmen from running, along with the way he converted certain boundaries into ones or twos, were worth 30 to 50 runs per day for his side. Many of the run-outs he achieved from cover, where because of his side-on position he only had one stump to aim at. Trevor Goddard, Bland's captain in 12 of his 21 Tests, said that "when Colin was patrolling the boundary, he would send these underarm throws whistling in. The batsmen wouldn't dare take two to him." Bland effected seven run-outs in 21 Tests; by comparison, Jonty Rhodes had eight in 52 Tests.

Bland's skills found full expression in the first Test in 1965 at Lord's, the hundredth between the two countries. England were 240 for four wickets in their first innings, just 40 runs behind and seeming set for a big total. Ken Barrington, one of the great English run-accumulators, was on 91 when he pushed the ball to mid-wicket and moved to take a single. Bland ran towards the square-leg umpire, reported *Wisden*, and "in one thrilling move-ment he scooped up the ball, swung round his body and threw down the stumps at the bowler's end". It was regarded as the turn-ing point of the tour and the series, which South Africa won 1-0. Bland performed similar acrobatics later in the innings to run out the England wicketkeeper Jim Parks, by throwing the ball between Parks's legs to hit the stumps. Over the match as a whole, wrote

Colin Bland: his aggressive middle-order batting and ability to rescue an innings were undeservedly overshadowed by his brilliant, spectacular fielding

Wisden, "the wonderful fielding of Bland, in particular, captured the imagination".

The veteran Rhodesian administrator Alwyn Pichanik recalled that "Bland's fielding was so outstanding that, even in the early days, spectators were attending matches in which he was playing just to see him field. He was also outstanding on the boundary because he had such a powerful arm, and his throws from 80 metres which travelled the whole distance at the level of the bails were nothing short of miraculous. He was such an athlete that he could have played any sport successfully. He decided to concentrate on cricket at an early age, after he had already been offered a rugby scholarship to Stellenbosch University, and he represented his country at hockey with great distinction."

However, it is with Bland the batsman that we are really concerned – and with a Test average of just under 50 from 21 Tests (two fewer than Graeme Pollock), he was more than worth his place in the powerful South African side of the mid-1960s. He was a naturally aggressive player, with a liking for lofting the ball to the boundary and for opening his innings with a six. At isolation in 1970, Bland was South Africa's leading six-hitter in Tests with 21. Ali recalls that Bland had a big-match temperament. "He was a strong player in front of the wickets, not a big cutter or sweeper or puller – mainly by driving, he scored most of his runs between cover and mid-wicket.

"Colin was also a thoughtful teammate. My first game for South Africa was in 1965 against Derbyshire at Chesterfield. It was a town serving a tough mining community, and I remember that the fast bowler Harold Rhodes was no-balled by umpire Syd Buller for throwing. The miners wanted to kill Buller. I was dismissed twice for five runs, once by Rhodes. If you had given me a gun that night … I was so depressed. I was dropped to 12th man for the next match against Yorkshire. On the bus down to the south for the match against Essex, Colin came to sit next to me. He saw that I was low, and he spoke to me about his own career. I can't remember what he said, but I do remember that he gave me a lot of confidence. We were good friends – whenever we went to Bulawayo, I would go to his house and have dinner with him and his wife."

In that Lord's Test in 1965, Bland shared with Graeme Pollock an important partnership of 80 in 95 minutes, after South Africa had been struggling at 75 for three. In the second innings, he came in with the score at 68 for three wickets – effectively 10 for three, taking into account the first-innings deficit – and put on 50 runs with Ali to help South Africa to a lead of 190. England were struggling in the end to save the game.

In the second Test, Bland did little with the bat as Pollock made 125 and South Africa won by 94 runs. In the third and final Test, however, he contributed a series-winning century. After the two sides were separated by just six runs in the first innings, South Africa were struggling at 123 for three in the second innings when Bland joined Ali. They put together another important partnership of 141 runs. Ali was 70 not out overnight – and went out first ball when play resumed after the Sunday rest day. When Bland was the eighth man out, he had seen his side's total increase by 244 runs while he was at the wicket. "With a patience that must have irked all his natural inclinations," wrote *Wisden*, "Bland resisted conscientiously the urge to put the ball in the air for the best part of his innings of 127. When he passed his century he could no longer tolerate the imposition of restraint and, enjoying good luck as he hit with abandon, he recorded the highest individual score of the series. His eleventh-hour success raised him to second place in South Africa's Test averages – 47.66 from 286 runs." Ali remembers that Bland did loft the ball during the innings – at one stage Brian Statham caught him off Fred Titmus inside the ropes, but Statham then ran over the boundary, and Bland got six runs instead of being out. The match was drawn, and so South Africa won the series.

In a star-studded side, Bland in 1965 was spoken of in the same breath as the Pollock brothers and Eddie Barlow. Yet he had been a slow starter, after a quiet beginning to his Test career five years earlier. He first came to the attention of the selectors when he made 91 for Rhodesia against the New Zealand tourists in the 1961–62 season, and was selected for the Test series. (In those days Rhodesia, now Zimbabwe, played as a province in the South African Currie Cup and their players qualified for Springbok selection.)

Although he played in all five Tests against New Zealand, his best score was 42 in nine innings, at an average of 22.77. His selection for Trevor Goddard's side to tour Australia in 1963–64 was therefore a surprise and widely questioned, and he did not play in the first Test.

In the second Test at Melbourne, though, his maiden Test 50 was the second-highest score (to Eddie Barlow's 109) in South Africa's first innings of 274. He followed that with another two half-centuries in the third Test, and in the fifth he scored his maiden Test century – 126 in five and a half hours. The Springboks were criticised for slow batting generally – but, as *Wisden* remarked, "the careful play of both sides reflected the fact that the series depended on this match". In six Test innings in Australia, Bland scored 367 runs at 61.16, thus cementing his place in the side – though his achievement was overshadowed in the series by the batting of Barlow and Pollock.

Bland was an automatic choice for the 1964–65 series against England in South Africa. England won the first Test in Durban by an innings. "They were overwhelmingly superior," said *Wisden*, "on a pitch which took spin early in the match, due, in part, to the shortage of grass. England were rather fortunate, not only to win the toss, but to find conditions so suitable to them. The South African batsmen had little answer to the spin of Allen and Titmus who shared 13 wickets, and their own attack was not the right type for such a pitch." Bland alone did well under these circumstances, top-scoring with 68 in South Africa's follow-on innings (Barlow made 0 and so did Pollock – the only duck of his Test career).

In the second Test in Johannesburg, South Africa followed on 214 runs behind. When Bland came to the wicket with the score in the second innings on 109 for four, South Africa still needed another 105 runs just to avoid the innings defeat. Bland scored a match-saving "magnificent century, using his feet to kill the menace of Allen and Titmus". He made a career-best 144 not out (including two massive sixes); while he was at the wicket 227 runs were scored in a total of 336. Only two other batsmen made or passed 50: Goddard (50) and Pollock (55).

In his next five Test innings, Bland made 78, 64, 55, 38 not out and 48. He finished the 1964–65 series with 572 runs at an average of 71.50 – well ahead of the 459 runs at 57.37 by the next best South African batsman, Graeme Pollock. Compared with this form, Bland himself said he was not at his best in the 1965 series in England, described above – but 18 months later he was still regarded as an automatic selection for the 1966–67 Test series against Australia.

Bland failed to score (only the second duck of his Test career) as South Africa crashed to 41 for five in the first innings of the first Test at the Wanderers, and managed a creditable 32 in the record-breaking second innings of 620. Then he badly damaged his knee while fielding a ball on the boundary, marked in those days by a low picket fence. He fell on the fence (this was the incident that caused its replacement by a rope), played no further part in the match, and never played Test cricket again.

Bland continued to play first-class cricket for another seven years. In the season after his knee injury, he made 197 in about three hours in a low-scoring match for Rhodesia against Border. Alwyn Pichanik regarded this as the best innings of Bland's career. Towards the end of his career he moved from the outfield and the covers to become an outstanding slip fielder.

Talented and dedicated, Bland was not as spectacular a batsman as Pollock, or as moody a personality as Richards, or as visibly self-confident as Barlow. His consistency with the bat, though, speaks for itself: only five other South African batsmen have achieved a higher Test average. His batting would surely have achieved more recognition if it had not been eclipsed by his fielding, which was uniquely spectacular and effective.

"I live for cricket," he said once. "I'd play every day if I could."

Colin Bland
Born 5 April 1938
International career: 1961–1966

	M	Inns	NO	Runs	HS	Avg	SR	100	50	Conv
Tests	21	39	5	1 669	144*	49.08	45*	3	9	25.00
First-class	131	219	28	7 249	197	37.95		13	34	27.65
List A	4	4	0	138	69	34.50		0	1	0.00

PART THREE

WHAT MIGHT
HAVE BEEN

By Krish Reddy

5

Ahmed Deedat

K waZulu-Natal has been fortunate in producing some fine strokeplayers. In the 1940s and 1950s we had players of the calibre of Davidson Chellan and "Shorty" Docrat, and close on their heels came Ahmed Deedat, who took over from where his predecessors left off, going on to carve a niche for himself in the annals of South African cricket as a batsman of the highest pedigree.

Short in stature but compact in build, Deedat made excellent use of his feet and played with superb timing. He had a solid defence and an ability to play the ball late, with minimum but effective movement, the attributes of only the very best players. He would come down the wicket or go right back, using that space between the stumps and the batting crease to the maximum to play his shots, at times almost getting onto his toes to force the short-of-a-length ball away. He was not an overtly aggressive batsman, yet he could take an attack apart and dictate the pattern of play, and do it all with marvellous strokes, beautifully executed: the square cut slightly backward of point, a piercing cover or off drive and, a shot you don't often see these days, a firm push past the bowler on either side of the wicket for one or two runs off any ball short of a length that would have kept almost any other player quiet.

When in form, Deedat hit to all parts of the field but he did it with such quiet detachment and an almost apologetic air that he seemed to mesmerise the bowler into delivering long hops and full pitches. At his peak, his trick when being tied down was to make it seem as if he was going to advance down the wicket and drive. The bowler would drop short and in a flash Deedat would be stepping back and across to pull the ball firmly past mid-wicket. In watching him so often and playing with and against him, I learnt one important thing: that a bowler only bowled as well as he was allowed to.

Given responsibility when very young, Deedat was asked to lead teams at representative level with men playing under him who had greater experience and were much older. Yet not once did he lose control of a situation and this could simply be attributed to his dignity, his example and his immense knowledge of the game. As a captain, he was quiet but firm, bringing into his decisions the wealth of experience he had absorbed over the years of playing in the highest company. When he gave advice, it was short, to the point and very effective. He also had that wonderful quality of seeing the good in his fellow players and urging them to bring out their best. He commanded the respect of all those who played with and against him because of his scrupulous honesty and the impeccable standard he set as a cricketer.

That he was naturally talented there is no doubt, but he did not achieve all his success on talent alone. He worked very hard at the game, practising assiduously and giving full attention not only to batting but to fielding and bowling as well. Above all he was superbly fit. Let it be remembered that he once won the fielding award at an inter-provincial tournament. He was a more than capable medium pace bowler who could cut the ball both ways and, when required, he could be used as a stock bowler for long spells of sustained accuracy.

An uncoached player, he was self-taught, evolving a technique characterised by intelligent application of basic skills observed in others and much that he picked up through reading and thinking about the game. His batting creed was a disarmingly simple one based on the advice of the legendary Ted Chetty, under whose

Ahmed Deedat (third from right, middle row): an immensely gifted player in an era of vintage cricket

captaincy he played as a youngster: Watch your wicket and the runs will come.

Much of Deedat's cricket was played in Pietermaritzburg for the Young Natalians Cricket Club at the Fitzsimmons Road Sports Ground. The ground was a beautiful one, tree lined and nestling in the shadow of Mountain Rise. It was here that he gave pleasure to countless followers of cricket every summer with his attractive strokeplay. But, true to his generous nature, he spread his favours everywhere for he gave spectators the opportunity to marvel at his powers with the bat throughout our country and even away from our borders. Deedat represented Natal Indians regularly from 1953 to 1960, playing in three Christopher tournaments. His first tournament, while he was still a schoolboy, saw him score 104 against Western Province Indians in Cape Town in 1953, when he was awarded a bat for the most promising cricketer. Playing as a boy amongst men, he learnt his lessons quickly and absorbed them well. In Johannesburg in 1955 he was vice-captain to Dawood Seedat of Ladysmith and scored a brilliant 146 and an unbeaten 69 against Griqualand West, in addition to winning a bat as the best fielder in the tournament. He led Natal Indians in the 1958 tournament in Port Elizabeth, captaining a young side with commendable success and sharing the Christopher trophy with the powerful Transvaal team.

His good form in the 1955 tournament led to his selection for the South African Indian team in the then racial quadrangular tournament in Johannesburg, where he played in two matches, batting on three occasions and achieving a highest score of 22. He played with modest success but showed all the signs of a class player. In 1958 in Cape Town, in the last of the racial quadrangular tournaments, he was selected as vice-captain of the South African Indian side and played in all matches, batting six times for an aggregate of 210 runs at an average of 42.00. Against a powerful Malay side which included the redoubtable Eric Petersen, a fast medium bowler who achieved outstanding results on the tour of Kenya and East Africa, Deedat batted attractively, for 31 and 64. He topped a fine performance in the national tournament with a stylish undefeated century against the South African Bantus. Not surprisingly, he was adjudged, technically, to be the best batsman on view by sportswriters covering the event.

In 1956 the Kenyan Asians toured South Africa and played matches against all the provincial units in the country as well as three "Test" matches. Deedat represented a combined Natal side in

Durban and, although he failed in the first innings together with many of his fellow batsmen against the pace of GB Jhalla, he made amends by scoring an impressive back-to-the-wall 22 in the second innings when Natal lost by an innings. A very successful season culminated in his selection as 12th man for the national side in the third Test against the Kenyan Asians at Kingsmead in Durban. An injury to the captain, Basil D'Oliveira, led to his inclusion in the team on the morning of the match, which was reduced to one day, the two previous days having been washed out by torrential rain. In a low-scoring game in which South Africa led on the first innings, Deedat only scored six, a great pity, for the rain-affected wicket assisted the bowlers throughout and robbed spectators of seeing this delightful strokeplayer make runs.

Deedat's career reached its zenith when he was selected to represent a combined Non-European South African team to tour Kenya and the East African territories in August and September 1958. It was a well-deserved honour indeed, and he joined the ranks of other celebrated cricketers such as Basil D'Oliveira, Cecil Abrahams, John Neethling, Tiny Abed, Eric Petersen, Lobo Abed and Owen Williams. The South Africans lost the first match against the Kenyan Asians by five wickets but not before Deedat made his mark as a batsman of the highest quality by scoring a fine 75 and featuring in a century partnership with Sidney Solomon, the Cape opening bat. The three "Tests" were won overwhelmingly by the South Africans who played fine cricket throughout the tour, a remarkable achievement considering the unfamiliar conditions and the unseasonable time of the year.

Deedat played in all three "Tests" and in six completed innings scored 199 runs for an average of 33.17. The big matches brought out the best in him and it was in these that he most revealed his wonderful temperament and superb batting skills. In the first "Test" he scored a face-saving 38 in the first innings before he was unfortunately run out, and completed the match with a splendid double by making 59 in the second and featuring in a century partnership with Basil D'Oliveira, who went on to score 139. In the second "Test" these two were at it again when Deedat scored 66 and D'Oliveira 96, putting on 149 for the fourth wicket. The immense value of these innings cannot be overemphasised as they were played when the South Africans were in dire straits and Deedat's solid defence and polished strokeplay laid the foundations for the big match-winning scores which the team eventually compiled.

On his return home, he played for a Transvaal non-racial invitation XI captained by Basil D'Oliveira against a Transvaal white team which included Peter Walker, the Glamorgan cricketer who later went on to play for England. He scored a century and played some of the finest cricket of his life, as he himself recalled, and thus topped a glittering career with a singularly remarkable batting display. His final representative games were played for Northern Natal when he captained them on a goodwill tour of Rhodesia in 1964. The side played entertaining and attractive cricket and Deedat capped the team's success with a sparkling hundred in one match and a pleasing 70 in another.

It was a great pity that the wrangle between Southern and Northern Natal led to a rift between the two units in the early sixties – thus he was not afforded the opportunity of playing in the very first two non-racial tournaments in Johannesburg and Port Elizabeth. This was a most unfortunate period for he would have shown to a later generation what an immensely gifted player he was. Even when he gave up representative cricket he was still far and away the best batsman in the province. It was a tribute to his powers that selectors still tried, in vain, to persuade him to play "big" cricket again.

To talk to Ahmed Deedat about cricket was to evoke fond memories because it quickly became clear how very much he enjoyed the game. He was generous in his praise of others and characteristically modest about his own stirring deeds. He played in an era of vintage cricket and his batsmanship was like the very best spark-ling wine.

After retiring from cricket, Deedat kept fit by playing golf and tennis. He ran a flourishing pet shop, Julie's Tropical Fish, in Durban for a number of years. Very much in the prime of his life he was killed tragically at the age of 63 in August 1998. He was playing golf and was knocked over by a car while waiting to cross DLI Avenue – the road that intersects the Royal Durban Golf Course in Greyville.

6

Frank Roro

Born in Kimberley in 1908, an impressionably shy and young Frank Roro was introduced to the game of cricket by Hamilton Masiza. Educated at Healdtown, Lovedale and Fort Hare – strongholds of African sport in the Eastern Cape – Masiza trained as a teacher and became principal of the United Mission School in Kimberley. Masiza's involvement in the summer game was well known and all encompassing. He served as secretary and vice-president of the South African Bantu Cricket Board from 1932 to 1941, and then as president from 1941 to 1954. A more than capable cricketer himself, Masiza was the ideal mentor for Roro and the precocious youngster proved to be an attentive pupil and quick learner. Blessed with enormous natural ability, excellent hand-eye co-ordination and a hunger to score runs, the young Roro provided ample evidence that he was to become a batsman head and shoulders above his contemporaries in black cricket.

Having absorbed his cricketing lessons avidly, Frank Roro left Kimberley in 1931 and moved to the Transvaal, where he joined the Randfontein mine team. His reputation as an outstanding batsman was burgeoning but still had to be tested in the highly competitive cricket leagues sponsored by the Chamber of Mines in the gold mining regions on the Rand. Further successful stints of club cricket with Van Ryn Deep and Rand Leases led to veteran player Robbey Brooker persuading him to join his team, Crown Mines, where Roro's exploits with the bat were phenomenal. His form was awesome, mind-boggling even, and he amassed prolific match-winning scores for his latest club, compiling his runs at will on pitches that were not always too batsman friendly. His priceless run-scoring ability was reflected in scores of 228 against West Rand in 1940 and 304 against Main Reef in 1942. Feats such as these were extraordinary when one considers the primitive and testing ground and pitch conditions prevailing in black cricket at the time.

Roro made his debut for the Transvaal Bantu team in the 1933-34 season, scoring 97 not out against Border and 129 against Natal. During his tenure as a provincial cricketer for Transvaal, whom he captained from 1938 onwards, nine inter-provincial tournaments were played from 1933-34 to 1950-51. Transvaal won six of these, securing the NRC (Native Recruiting Commission) Trophy sponsored by the Chamber of Mines. Leading by example with the bat and setting the standard for good fielding as a more than capable slip fieldsman himself, Roro revealed a sound understanding of the game. He was tactically astute and his leadership style was firm yet undemonstrative. He was also deeply conscious of improving and extending the cricketing ability of his fellow players. Always well groomed and dressed immaculately in the appropriate cricketing attire, he was not only a leader but an idol as well.

Although African cricket has been poorly documented, there is enough evidence from scattered contemporary local black newspapers to reveal that, statistically, Roro's influence in Transvaal's supremacy was quite profound. He scored 114 against Border in 1937 and had a very productive 1938-39 tournament in Durban. In 1950 he made 102 not out in a total of 137 against Western Province; at this stage he was in his early forties. Unfortunately, more details cannot be garnered as match reporting was cursory, with little attention paid to individual scores when results were recorded. At some tournaments, reporting was fragmentary and scores given were incomplete. What must be remembered is that

Frank Roro (fourth from right, standing): whoever came close to him was a rather distant second

Roro scored his runs very quickly and in so doing provided his team with more than ample bowling time to dismiss their opponents and secure convincing victories. Because of the comparatively big scores that Transvaal compiled through Roro's contributions, close attacking fields could be set for long periods of time.

In addition to the African provincial tournaments, the Transvaal Africans played regularly against Indian and Coloured clubs and provincial teams. In 1936 a pioneering Johannesburg Inter-Race Board was formed and an annual inter-race league was inaugurated with the Bernard L Sigamoney Trophy at stake. Winning the title in 1938-39 and being joint winners in 1940-41, on both occasions under Roro's captaincy, the Transvaal Africans showed a high level of competitiveness against some very strong opposition. Between 1934 and 1951 Frank Roro scored well over 3 000 runs for the Transvaal Bantu team, which included 20 centuries, and a highest score of 228 against the Transvaal Coloureds. In all senior cricket he is reputed to have scored over 100 centuries with an average of over 100 per season. It is no small wonder that he was rightfully given the moniker "Dusty Bradman".

In 1951 the recently formed South African Cricket Board of Control (SACBOC) arranged the first of its four biennial national inter-race tournaments. It was played at the Natalspruit Indian Sports Ground in Johannesburg. The South African Coloureds, South African Indians and South African Bantus participated in two-day matches on a league basis with the Dadabhay Trophy as the victor's prize. Hitherto, Frank Roro's amazing feats had been confined to the limited cricketing milieu of his own race group with occasional forays against the Indians and Coloureds. In this tournament his prowess with the bat was going to be tested against some of the very best bowlers in the country. The Indians could boast of outstanding fast bowlers such as Tiny Abed and AFW Stephens, left-arm seamer "Foofy" Timol and the reputable leg-spinner Essop Jeewa; the Coloureds could field legendary all-rounder Basil Waterwick, very much in the Basil D'Oliveira mould, and penetrative paceman Ralph Simons. At the age of 43 Frank Roro was to reveal that he was no show pony in his own backyard.

Captaining his national side and batting with all the aplomb of the seasoned veteran he was, he scored 116, the first and only century in this very first Dadabhay National Inter-Race tournament. Roro was in total command as he unleashed an array of attractive strokes on both sides of the wicket. His innings helped his side gain a first innings win over their much more fancied opponents, the South African Indians. Another impressive innings of 66 against the South African Coloureds enabled him to compile a total of 192 runs in four innings at an average of 48.00 and to become the tournament's leading run-scorer. He batted at his accustomed position of number four in the order in making that 66. It was a little more than half his team's score of 127 in the first innings in which the redoubtable Basil Waterwick was in rampant bowling form, capturing eight wickets for 32 and an eventual match haul of 12 wickets. It was to be a more than fitting swansong for a veritable giant in the annals of black cricket. Faced with the sternest test that black cricket could offer him, he accepted the challenge with great decorum and held centre stage with the bravura reserved only for those with a special gift. At an age when most cricketers would have long since retired from competitive cricket, he showcased his incredible batting skills to a post-war generation. He was peerless, his batting technique was near flawless and his strokeplay was aesthetically pleasing. Whoever came close to him was a rather distant second. He wore the mantle of greatness with great humility and dignity.

When SJ Reddy, the editor of the now scarce South African Non-European Cricket Almanac of the mid-1950s, chose him retrospectively as one of his five Cricketers of the Year in recognition of his fabulous deeds as a batsman, he said the following about his modus operandi in his citation:

"Barely 5 ft 8 in in height, Roro does not allow his comparatively small physique to handicap him in stroke production. What he lacks in reach he makes up for by his perfect footwork and quick eye.

"He wields his willow with grace, power and soundness. His defence tells of the long study of the game. He is not averse to going to drive the fast bowlers, he employs the hook as a safe scoring stroke and delights the onlookers by the neat skill of his glance and general placing to the leg."

In 2002–03, when André Odendaal was working on his book *The Story of an African Game*, he cited editor Chris Day's *Developing Winners* in which Lawrence Mvumvu, the veteran Soweto player and administrator who played with Roro and was highly influenced by him, evokes fond and vivid memories of this cricketer extra-ordinaire and admirable gentleman:

"He was on the quiet side, soft spoken. At no time would he boast about his talent. Instead he was keen to help those who needed help. He was humble and dignified. I admired everything he did. He was graceful and unique when he was batting or bowling his off-spinners. He was as good as Eric Rowan or Bruce Mitchell, maybe even better. He played on atrocious wickets but kept playing straight and his shot placings were outstanding. He was very hungry for runs, and could bat for very long periods in difficult conditions and still managed to look graceful and fluent at all times. Watching Frank play cricket and the way he helped introverted and shy teen-agers like myself made me realise that cricket was to be my game."

Towards the latter part of 1999, through the initiative of Dr Ali Bacher and the then United Cricket Board of South Africa, Colin Bryden, as convener, was asked to form a selection committee to choose South Africa's 10 Cricketers of the Century. I was privileged to be a member of this committee, which also included the late Ken Funston, former Springbok; John Neethling, former SA Cricket Board of Control international; Dave Richardson, the former Proteas wicketkeeper; and Zim Lubatani, the former South African Africans captain. Frank Roro was a unanimous choice as one of the 10 South African cricketers. The other nine were: Aubrey Faulkner, Dudley Nourse, Hugh Tayfield, Basil D'Oliveira, Eric Petersen, Graeme Pollock, Mike Procter, Barry Richards and Allan Donald. When Nelson Mandela was informed of Roro's selection, he responded spontaneously with a beaming smile and said: "Roro, yes, he was legendary."

Frank Roro died at the age of 63 in 1971, his passing away unheralded. Only a small coterie of black cricketers and his family were present at his funeral. Sadly, recognition for Roro came long afterwards, in the late 1990s, when the Frank Roro Oval was estab-lished in Galeshewe, a thriving cricketing community. His son was invited to the millennium Test at Newlands in Cape Town by the United Cricket Board of South Africa to accept a commemorative medal honouring his father as one of South Africa's 10 Cricketers of the Century.

Colin Bryden, in an article in the *Sunday Times* in November 1999, fittingly wrote: "The story of Frank Roro is one of shame for South African cricket. An extraordinary batsman, he was doomed to play most of his cricket in relative obscurity and usually in inferior company."

PART FOUR

SOMETHING TO PROVE

G ary Kirsten's first Test was the Boxing Day match at Melbourne in 1993. Jacques Kallis came into the national side two years later in the Durban Test against England. For the next nine years they formed the backbone of South Africa's batting. Kirsten's international career lasted just over a decade; Kallis played an amazing 166 Tests in 18 years.

Gary was the first outstanding South African batsman after the period of isolation that ended in 1991, and in many ways he was a pioneer: he went where none of his countrymen of any era had been before. From a batting perspective, he helped lay the foundation for an era where South Africa would consistently be ranked first in Test cricket.

Kirsten was the first South African to play in a hundred Test matches, and the first man from any country to score a century against each of the nine Test-playing countries. For some years he held the South African record for the most consecutive Tests played (53), the most Test runs (7 289) and centuries (21). He equalled Daryll Cullinan's record individual Test score (275), and was the first South African to make three double-centuries.

After South Africa's readmission in 1991, Kirsten was the first to score a double-ton in a Test innings; the first to make a century in each innings of the same Test; and the first to carry his bat through a completed innings (only Bernard Tancred, Jimmy Zulch, Trevor Goddard and Jackie McGlew had done this before isolation began in 1970).

It was only in 2012 that the cricket world began to talk about a South African team without Jacques Kallis. For his batting alone, with an average of 55.37 in Tests and 44.36 in one-day internationals, he ranks among the all-time greats from any country. He is in 11th place on the list of highest career averages in Tests, ahead of his great contemporaries Sachin Tendulkar, Brian Lara and Ricky Ponting. Add his bowling contribution (292 Test wickets at 32 runs each), as well as 200 catches, and there is only one other cricketer in history in the same class as Kallis: the West Indian Sir Garfield Sobers.

Towards the end of his career, it seemed the South African authorities were expecting less bowling, if at all, from Kallis as they attempted to prolong his batting career. He has said he has never been particularly interested in statistics, but the prospect of overtaking the record of Tendulkar's 51 centuries in Tests must surely have gained his attention. In the event, Kallis retired with 45 hundreds, the second-highest total in history, in a career that started six years after Tendulkar's. Of the 11 all-time great players who have scored 10 000 Test runs, the Sri Lankan Sangakkara has scored centuries most frequently (one every 3.47 Tests), followed by Sunil Gavaskar (3.67) and Kallis (3.68), ahead of Brian Lara (3.85) and Sachin Tendulkar (3.92).

In December 2013, Jacques announced his retirement from Test cricket but made it clear he intended to continue in the one-day side in order to play in the next World Cup in February–March 2015. But his one-day form at the end of 2013 had not been good – just 76 runs in four matches against India and Pakistan. In July 2014 he made just five runs in three innings against Sri Lanka, and decided his heart was no longer in it. The 2015 World Cup had turned out to be a bridge too far, and Kallis retired with immediate effect.

Thus came to an end two decades of South African cricket history – a period that deserves to be marked as the Kirsten-Kallis era.

It's easy to forget in 2015, at a time when South Africa has several modern batsmen with a Test average of 50-plus or in the high 40s – Kallis, Graeme Smith, AB de Villiers, Hashim Amla, Faf du Plessis – that it was not always so. In 1997, after more than five years of Test matches since readmission, all the leading South African batsmen of that period – Hansie Cronje, Daryll Cullinan, Lance Klusener, Brian McMillan, Andrew Hudson, Jonty Rhodes – had a batting average below 40. Even Kepler Wessels, who returned to international cricket with his home country in 1992 five years after his career with Australia ended, averaged only 38 for South Africa. In 83 years of Test cricket up to 1970, the only South African batsmen who achieved a Test average higher than 50 were Graeme Pollock (60.97), Dudley Nourse (53.81) and Barry Richards (72.57, though in only four Tests).

Kirsten and Kallis raised the bar. They established new levels of confidence and expectation for modern South African batsmen. They ensured that big individual scores and partnerships were no longer a rarity. They proved able to absorb pressure from the best bowling attacks, and often to dominate them. They were required to perform on all kinds of wickets in all the major cricket-playing countries – unlike the pre-1970 South African batsmen, who had the opportunity to play only against England, Australia and New Zealand.

An illustration of their importance to the team was their contribution at Old Trafford in July 1998. South Africa made 552 for five, and at the heart of the innings was the 238-run partnership between Kirsten and Kallis – a South African second-wicket Test record and at that point the country's best for any wicket since isolation. Jacques made 132, and Gary's 210 was his maiden Test double-century. He batted ten hours and 50 minutes, the longest Test innings ever by a South African at the time. "Even Bruce Mitchell and Jackie McGlew," said *Wisden*, "never matched this for stickability."

7

Gary Kirsten

"The first time I really met Gary," recalls Ali, "was when he came to the United Cricket Board offices in 1993, before going to join the national team in Australia. I have never seen anyone so enthusiastic and keen at being given the opportunity."

Gary had not expected to be part of the team. "I'd had a fairly good first-class year, and there was talk of me being selected for the series against India and Australia, but I wasn't selected for that initial tour. And then Brian McMillan got injured in a game at the Melbourne Cricket Ground. Just prior to that, they'd had a Madonna concert and the field wasn't in the greatest condition. I'm not quite sure how Brian hurt himself on the field, but people said to me, 'You made your entry to international cricket on the back of a Madonna concert.'

"As a sportsman, you get a level of performance where you wonder if you can go to the next level – and now that moment had arrived. I hadn't thought I'd get even close.

"My first Test was at the MCG, Boxing Day, 1993. It was rained out as a draw and I didn't really fire at all. My second Test was the famous win at Sydney. That for me was the breaking of the ice – I didn't play very well, but it gave me belief that I could play at this level."

In the low-scoring, slow-scoring but thrilling Sydney Test over New Year 1994, Kirsten certainly played well enough: he top-scored with 67 as South Africa made 169; only two other batsmen reached double figures. In the second innings Kirsten made the second-highest score with 41 out of 239. Australia were set a winning target of just 117 runs, with more than a day to get them. Near the close of play on day four, an Australian win seemed inevitable when they had reached 51 for one wicket – but then Fanie de Villiers took three quick wickets for the addition of just five runs, and the home side were rather more unsteadily placed at the close on 63 for four.

"They needed only about 50 runs the next morning and time wasn't an issue," recalled South Africa's champion fast bowler Allan Donald. "But we said we'd come back and have a fresh start in the morning. The wicket was getting slower and lower, and it was just starting to reverse-swing a little. We went to the Aussie dressing-room for a drink after play on the fourth day – we would always have an end-of-day drink in the batting side's change-room – and Mark Waugh said something I will never forget. 'Just put a couple of plebs in there, toss it up, and let's get this match over with,' he said. He meant that we should let guys that don't bowl too often have a bowl. It's things like those that you don't forget.

"I went back to the hotel and I said to my wife that we probably had an outside chance, but we'd need a bit of luck on the final day. Kepler Wessels called us all into a meeting, although he wasn't going to be on the field on day five, because of a broken thumb, and Hansie Cronje was the acting captain. Kepler said that if, in the first hour, we bowled anything like what we were capable of bowling, and squeezed them for runs, we could win it."

Going into the final day, Ali remembers, De Villiers was reported in the media as saying something along the lines of: "Australia, please believe me, we can win this Test."

Did Gary think they could win going into the final day? "I think the night before was crucial. Our attitude was very positive. One thing I've always found with SA cricket, it's our never-say-die attitude. We fight to the death. That's been one of our characteristics."

With his second ball of the morning, Donald bowled Allan Border, an event especially unsettling to the batting side because the batsman had not offered a shot. "I thought that could be a turning point," said Donald. "That's when we really felt we could win," says Gary.

It was indeed the turning point. The Australians lost all confidence and crashed to 111 all out – a thrilling five-run victory for South Africa, with De Villiers taking six for 43.

Kirsten was still very much a new boy in the side. "Of course, this was only my second Test. As was traditional, after the match we went into the Australian dressing-room. I was a bit sheepish, didn't really know anyone, wasn't sure about this space. We did have this feeling that Australia was kind of above us, and they were the guys to look up to. So I walk into this change-room, the last one to come in. Everyone's sitting in a circle, both teams, a couple of beers out. And there's one seat left, and that's next to Allan Border. And I thought, I'm going to make the most of this opportunity. I sat with Allan Border for the better part of an hour and I must have asked him 35 to 40 questions, just about Test cricket. And that was one of the most valuable hours I've ever had with anyone – a hardened Test cricketer. It was one of the best pieces of learning I've ever had – he gave me a snapshot of what Test cricket is all about. We still connect, even today."

South Africa lost the third Test in Adelaide and drew the series. That was followed by a Benson & Hedges World Series ODI tournament involving South Africa, Australia and New Zealand. Kirsten scored 51 and 55 in his first five innings, and then, in front of 70 000 people at Melbourne, he scored his maiden century in only his sixth ODI. He opened with his half-brother Peter and they put on 53 together, with Gary "cutting fiercely and driving well".

Kirsten was in a team that kept making history. His first Test series was also the first between South Africa and Australia in 23 years, the first in Australia for 30 years. Next on the programme was the eagerly awaited tour of England – the first official contact between the two countries since 1965.

Before the first Test at Lord's, former England captain Tony Lewis wrote in the *Sunday Telegraph* (24 July 1994) that the emphasis on the celebration of South Africa's return was wrong and insensitive.

"The publicity and all the chatter which has surrounded the Test match at Lord's prove that very few British people understand the messages which have been emanating from SA for the past few years," said Lewis. "The publicity is all about the old days. We have been told how many a Test career was blighted by the 29-year break in cricket relations and wherever you look there is a picture of Barry Richards, Mike Procter, the Pollock brothers or Eddie Barlow. There is nothing wrong with appreciating the high skills of these cricketers but the headline for this match should be that at Lord's we are not seeing the return of South Africa, we are seeing the first Test played at Lord's by a new South Africa."

Lewis wrote that "having witnessed something of the years of endeavour, seen brave sponsors like Baker's Biscuits, Castle Lager, Nissan and others pour resources into multi-racial cricket, to see 'the miracle country' take the field for the first time in England was very special". As Mark Nicholas, the former Hampshire captain, put it: "These men are the standard-bearers of a new, four-month-old nation."

In South Africa's first innings at Lord's, Kirsten opened and lost both Hudson and Cronje cheaply. He was joined by Kepler Wessels with the score at 35 for two. They put on 106 together. Christopher Martin-Jenkins described Gary as "playing solidly in his correct, no-frills manner". He made 72 in three and a half hours, including 12 fours, "mainly well-timed strokes off either foot between backward point and mid-off". Then he tried to drive Graeme Hick but mistimed the shot and spooned a catch to the covers.

Barry Richards felt that "it was Kepler Wessels's stand with Gary Kirsten, when the Test was precariously balanced, that epitomised

Gary Kirsten: he steadily accumulated runs and records, and became the rock on which South Africa's batting could flourish

what this team is all about. It was only when these two were together that South Africa were able to reach a stage of domination. If you wanted one word to sum these South Africans up, it would be 'tough'."

Wessels made 105, and coach Mike Procter celebrated by waving the new South African flag from the balcony of the pavilion. This was against the rules, which prohibited the waving of any banners or flags at Lord's, but nobody dared to stop him and South Africa reached a respectable 244 for six at the end of day one.

The team went on to make 357, and at the end of the second day had England battling at 141 for seven; the next morning, they were all out for 180. Gary made a useful 44 in South Africa's second-innings 278. Even though he was stumped off Hick, wrote Colin Bryden, "he was using his feet to get to the pitch of the ball rather than to try to slam it to the boundary. He has enjoyed an excellent match." Scyld Berry noted that "he put the impetus into South Africa's first and second innings with his square cutting and driving".

Berry continued: "In keeping with their new emblem the protea, South African cricket has burst into bloom, and so agreeable is this new flower that not for a long time has the world of Test cricket seen such a joyous sight ... it was the sheer energy of South African cricket which has impressed England most, such as when Gary Kirsten brought off a run-out which was perfection of its kind ... running from short leg to deep mid-on, he picked up and threw down the bowler's stumps as Angus Fraser went for a third. He had only a preparatory look-round, a few strides before picking up, to guide him."

England were blasted out for 99 in their second innings, giving South Africa a famous victory by 356 runs inside four days. But the Leeds Test ended in a draw, thanks to Gary making 65 ("solid, untroubled and uncomplicated") and brother Peter 104; and the final Test at the Oval (Gary made 2 and 0) was won by England. This was the match when Devon Malcolm took nine for 57.

Gary's first Test century came the next year (1995), in November against England (their first tour to South Africa in 31 years) in Johannesburg. South Africa batted first and made 332, and a third of those runs came from Kirsten. He batted for five hours and 50 minutes for 110, and was fifth out with the score on 260. His achievement was overshadowed, though, by Mike Atherton's remarkable unbeaten 185. England were set a target of 479, and a win for South Africa seemed only a matter of time. But Atherton defied the South African bowlers for nearly two days to extract for England a draw from the most unlikely situation.

Almost exactly another year later, in November 1996 in India, Kirsten became only the third South African to make two centuries (102 and 133) in a Test, after Alan Melville and Bruce Mitchell. He played an important part as South Africa levelled the series, in front of a daily Calcutta crowd of 50000. The pitch was true and the outfield fast. In the South African first innings, Hudson and Kirsten put on 236 for the first wicket, the second-highest opening stand in South Africa's history.

In the second innings Gary shared in another mammoth partnership: 212 runs for the second wicket with Daryll Cullinan, also a record. The two partnerships were worth 448 runs – 56 per cent of the team's total in the match. India's eventual target was 467 in just over four sessions, and South Africa won by 329 runs. However, Gary's achievement in a Test was again somewhat overshadowed, this time by Lance Klusener's astonishing eight wickets for 64 in the second Indian innings and by a sensational first-innings knock from Mohammad Azharuddin, who reached his century in 74 deliveries.

Gary maintained his rhythm for annually knocking off milestones. In October 1997 he scored an unbeaten 100, thus becoming only the fourth South African to carry his bat in a Test – that is, opening the innings and not being dismissed, with all ten wickets falling. It happened in the third Test at Faisalabad in Pakistan, against the formidable seam and swing of Wasim Akram and Waqar Younis.

Batting first, South Africa were 30 for four and then 99 for seven at lunch. Then, reported *Wisden*, "Kirsten, bristling with scratchy, scuffling determination, was joined by Pat Symcox, who can really irritate bowlers. His 81, from 94 balls, dominated their stand of 124," a crucial contribution to the total of 236. Again, however, there was a distraction to an achievement by Gary, when a googly bowled by Mushtaq "slipped under the bat of Symcox and passed between off and middle stump". The bails were not disturbed, and so Symcox survived. He then took three wickets for eight runs as Pakistan were shot out for 92 in their second innings to lose the Test by 53 runs and the series 1-0.

The great Australian bowler Shane Warne has said that, of all South African batsmen, he found Gary and Jacques Kallis the most difficult to dislodge. "Warne got me out a few times," says Gary, "but I had some success against him. There is a bonus to being a left-hander. He was outstanding against right-handers – his exploitation of the rough on day four and day five when he was bowling to right-handers was remarkable. But we left-handers could get away with it a bit more, because it was easier to stick a pad out there and you couldn't really be given out lbw. That was the nature of my play – I could play the patience game." Kirsten was dismissed five times by Warne, but scored 267 runs off him at an average of 53.40. Of batsmen to whom Warne bowled 600 or more balls, only Lara (71.57) had a better average against him.

"It wasn't the variety of Warne's balls, it was the package," says Kirsten. "He bowled a great leg-spinning delivery – whereas a lot of guys rely on their variation, I don't think he needed to. He had the flipper, but once he injured his shoulder the flipper was not so much of a weapon. His main ball was a high-quality leg-spinner, simple as that. And then he used to bowl this ball to me in one-day cricket, a slider. It took me ages to work out what he was doing.

He bowled it with a leg-spinning action, held the ball with the seam – it would spin, but it would spin on the shiny part of the leather. I started to pick it."

Gary believes his best batting against Warne was in the Test match in Adelaide in 1998, when he got 77 and 108. "We were trying to get a good lead in the second innings – so I was trying to take him on a bit, and I was able to get hold of him a few times. That was the most aggressive I was against Warne. Australia was always the main enemy. It wasn't my best Test knock, but it was certainly my best against Australia."

In that match South Africa set Australia a target of 361 to win, and Gary's total of 185 runs in the match had been crucial in setting his side up. Australia scraped to a draw, hanging on with 227 for eight at the close. Again, an outstanding Kirsten batting performance was eclipsed, this time by the controversy that erupted when Mark Waugh appeared to be out hit-wicket, but was not given out. It is worth quoting in detail some of the comments on this incident.

"Waugh received a Pollock lifter which hit him on the arm," reported *Wisden*, "and walked away as if in disgust; as he did so, his bat brushed the stumps and dislodged a bail. The South Africans appealed vehemently, even though he had clearly finished his stroke and could not therefore have been given out hit-wicket under Law 35. The umpires prolonged the agony, consulting the third umpire, Steve Davis. South Africa's misery was compounded when Adam Bacher, at short leg, dropped Waugh next ball. In fact, Waugh was dropped four times, three of them by Bacher."

There were conflicting views from those who played in the game: Shaun Pollock: "Waugh summed it up when he said his arm went numb and he lost control of the bat. If a batsman loses control and hits the stumps, that's out. That was a crucial blow for us. We weren't sure what had happened at first. The ball looped up to gully. So we were appealing for the catch. We weren't sure whether it had hit his arm only or his glove as well. It went to the third umpire, and the guys in the dressing-room were signalling that he was out. Then the verdict came back as not out."

Stuart MacGill: "When he got hit, knowing the way he carried himself, all of us saw him playing the stroke and then just sort of flopping around and carrying on a bit because it hurt. None of us really thought there was an issue until the South Africans raised it. And then we were a bit nervous because we didn't know how the umpires would respond. I don't believe it was controversial at all."

Ian Healy: "It was well after the shot and it wasn't part of the shot when the wicket was broken. I was of the opinion it was the right decision."

Jacques Kallis: "I was in the covers, and I thought it was, umm, very close to being out. I don't think too many of us were too interested in inviting him out for dinner after that. There were harsh words. But if you're going to play like that, if you're not going to walk in those circumstances, then you must expect the opposition to come hard at you."

Ali remembers the two former captains of Australia who were commentating on TV at the time, Bill Lawry and Richie Benaud, arguing about whether Waugh was out (Lawry thought he was).

A year after Gary's Adelaide feat, he equalled the highest score made by a South African in Tests. In making 275 in Durban in 1999, matching Daryll Cullinan's score against New Zealand the previous February, Gary also produced the second longest Test innings of all time. He had come into the match against England in the third Test at Kingsmead under pressure: his six previous Test scores were 40, 12, 13, 15, 2 and 11, and his average had sunk below 40.

South Africa had to follow on, and when Gary came to the wicket in the second innings the deficit was 210. South Africa began the final morning on 251 for four, just 41 runs ahead and with England scenting victory. Kirsten was on 126, having scored all but three of his runs when he batted the entire fourth day. He batted on three days of the Test. When he was eventually dismissed, 14 hours 38 minutes and 209 overs after he came to the crease with the score on 0, the total was 572 for seven. His wicket was taken by the part-time spinner Mark Butcher, just after 5pm on the final day.

"Mark Butcher bowled an off-spinner round my legs," says Gary. "I tried to knock it for one through mid-wicket and I got bowled. It was a lollipop delivery – but you have to remember the context of the innings. In many ways, at that stage I didn't care what was happening, I was so exhausted. But I also had saved my Test career, because if I hadn't got runs then I would have been dropped – rightly so. And we also saved the Test match after following on. So there was a much bigger picture than me breaking the record. People say, 'How could you get out to that delivery?' And I say, 'You can get out to any delivery.' And I virtually couldn't stand on my feet, I was so tired. We batted for three and a half days of that Test match. And I'll never forget the New Year game at Newlands – us going out to bat three days later, and those England bowlers were absolutely exhausted. And I thought, this is going to be a time to cash in."

Cash in the South Africans did: Gary made 80 in a first innings total of 421 and England were beaten by an innings and 37 runs.

South Africa were now two Tests up with one to play. The final Test at Centurion was "apparently reduced to the deadliest of finishes," wrote Neil Manthorp in *Wisden*. "Following three consecutive playless days, the match was brought back to life by the captains. For the first time in Test cricket, innings were forfeited and this produced a memorable, entertaining climax. When play resumed on day five, with South Africa still batting in their first innings, the many hundreds of travelling English supporters and a few hundred hardy locals had every reason to expect the worst. What they were treated to was a gripping finale that saw England win with five balls and two wickets remaining.

"Five months after the match, however, came the bitterness of deceit when Hansie Cronje, South Africa's captain, admitted receiving R53 000 and a leather jacket from a bookmaker, who had urged him to initiate a positive result, rather than let the match peter out as a draw. At the King Commission inquiry into match-fixing, he insisted that his motives were 'for the good of cricket', but the fact that financial reward formed a part of his motivation tainted the match for ever. History would also record that it was the first Test in which 'fixing' was proven."

Gary played in three World Cups, but the most memorable was in 1999, when South Africa lost the semi-final in the last over to Australia, after a mix-up between Lance Klusener and Allan Donald. "A lot of people say that the 1999 semi-final at the World Cup in England must have been the greatest disappointment of my career," he says. "I don't look at it like that. That semi-final was the greatest game of cricket I've ever been involved in. There has to be a winner and a loser. I just see it as a privilege to have been involved in that game. I think for us, the disappointment that will always sit with me was that 1999 was the best chance we had to win a World Cup. We were playing as good a quality of cricket as we could ever have been playing – it was a great team, we had an 80 per cent win ratio over the previous three years, the team was settled.

"There was always going to be massive pressure on that semi-final. It didn't flow, it was a game where there wasn't a winner. Someone was going to lose it. Nobody was really winning it. The Australians didn't play particularly well and neither did we. It was bizarre in many ways how it ended, because it would have been fitting if Lance had won it for us.

"We had a great team. Under Bob Woolmer, we had a great four-year period – he brought new thinking into our one-day cricket, creative thinking, and we really built a solid one-day base. We went around the world and we just blitzed it."

Another kind of disaster forced the side out of the 2003 World

Cup. In a key group match against Sri Lanka, the batsmen on the field needed to be told what they had to score to win the match. Nicky Boje was sent onto the field to convey the correct information – but the umpire prevented him from communicating with the batsmen, and South Africa were out of the tournament. "It wasn't a management mess-up, though we picked it up late," says Gary. "We've had some bizarre things happening in World Cups."

Choking was real, says Gary: "It became a factor, without a doubt. It wasn't a conscious thing, it became a subconscious thing. Steve Waugh once said the team that panics the least wins. It's not as if one side has got it together. But there's a bit of a legacy in the South African side – every young player comes in and there's that dark mist. You can accept it, or you can pretend it doesn't exist. Michael Jordan, the greatest basketball player of all time, said that 'people forget that I failed a lot of the time'. In fact the Proteas have achieved a remarkable story – we have been in the top three in the world since our reintroduction to world cricket."

Gary believes that if teams want to do well at the World Cup, they need to enjoy themselves more. Sometimes the accusation of "choking" is inappropriate. It shouldn't really be applied merely because there is a close and exciting contest where one side edges ahead at the end. In such cases an individual may crack under the pressure – a dropped catch, a misjudged drive – but this is part of the game. Choking is only a useful concept if it is applied to a team that contrives to lose when it is seemingly entrenched in a winning position, and when it has in theory played well enough to remove pressure from itself at the end.

Choking, then, is collapsing under the weight of an *absence* of pressure. Gary Kirsten understood this very well.

Gary has interesting things to say about Herschelle Gibbs, his most frequent opening partner in Tests and ODIs. "He fulfilled his potential in many ways. We opened the batting for the better part of five years and I loved opening with him. We were different personalities and different kinds of player, so we complemented each other. When you walk out to bat for your country, you cross the rope together, you are the best of mates. We became very close because of that. We had only each other to turn to. And that's the beauty of sport, isn't it?"

Gary's success was based on hard work as much as talent. "I was always a keen practiser. I was brought up in a cricketing family and there were a couple of non-negotiables. One was that you have to score a hundred, and you have to learn quickly how to do that. That was drummed into me from the age of 10. The other was that you have to practise. There are no short-cuts. You have to hit lots of balls. I never lost my enthusiasm for practice. I found the winter a great opportunity to tap into skill work. For example, I spent many hours one winter with Duncan Fletcher, my coach at Western Province, trying to hit the ball straighter on the on side. If you want to change your technique a bit, it's going to take a whole winter to do it."

Who were the best bowlers Gary faced?

"Glenn McGrath was the best bowler I ever faced, by a distance. He was a great bowler to left-handers. I found him the most difficult. I opened the batting, and he had the complete fast bowler's package. He had enough pace, he was tall, he bowled really tight lines to left-handers, made you play a lot of balls. He had good aggression about him as an individual, hated going for runs. If there was one bowler in the world I battled against more than any other, it would have been him, without a doubt. Left-handers love to leave the ball in Test cricket, but he stopped you leaving the ball. He made you play. He didn't swing it, but he had a good bounce. He was very similar to Shaun Pollock, actually – came very close to the crease and made you play a lot of balls. But the advantage he had over Shaun was that he was taller, with a higher action, so he got more natural bounce than Shaun did.

"The fastest bowler I faced was Shoaib Akhtar. He was the most fearsome bowler I ever came across. I didn't like facing him at all. He was very quick, with an action where you couldn't see the ball early. In some ways he was a double personality as a bowler."

A few years after retirement, Gary went into coaching, with conspicuous success – firstly with India and then with South Africa.

The great Indian batsman Sachin Tendulkar said Gary was the best coach he ever had. "Coaching is a leadership story in many ways," says Gary. "I had a lot of coaches in my career, and I was always very attentive to what they were saying. I wanted to package the stuff that really did make a difference to me. I felt a responsibility because I had a lot to offer after an 11-year international career."

He understood it was important to break into the Indian culture, and to be accepted in that culture. "I asked Sachin: what are your expectations of me as a coach? What do you want from me? He'd had a tumultuous period with Greg Chappell, he was talking about retiring and he wasn't interested in playing any more. And he said to me, 'I just want you to be my friend.' It was a very powerful thing to say, though I didn't understand then exactly what he meant.

"But after we'd won the World Cup in 2011, I was walking to my hotel room at 2am or 3am. The game had ended quite late, and of course there were festivities at the ground, we went out afterwards for a party with the team. Sachin's wife Angeline saw me in the hotel, stopped me and said, 'Gary, I just want to have a word with you. You're probably going to leave in a few days and I probably won't see you, so I just want to thank you for what you've done for Sachin. It's been the happiest three years of his life.' In those three years he got 18 international hundreds, and he played some of the best cricket he's ever played.

"I don't believe coaching at the highest level is about the technical side. That's very small – 5 per cent of the work. Technical coaching should be done away from a cricket match. It should be done with younger players. You should be honing skills at a much younger age than when a guy has signed on as a professional.

"Coaching is leadership, it's man-management. There's a lot of strategic and tactical stuff, and that's where I have grown a lot. There's not a lot of tactical work at Test-match level, it's more about courage and resilience, knowing your game and where you want to hit the ball."

Gary elaborated his ideas on leadership in an interview with Cricinfo in March 2014:

"When I was with the Indian team, as with the South African team, there was enough talent in both to know that they should be the best in the world. I think there is a subtleness to understanding what needs to be done to drive people towards a goal and drive them in a way that everyone goes in formation. It is a leader's responsibility to make that work. Many teams have lots of talent but the team underperforms. That is what I love about coaching in a team sport: there is a variety of people as individuals, and it is your responsibility to move everyone in the right direction.

"Socialising is a very dangerous space. A game ends and everyone goes out to enjoy themselves. As a coach, you can't be seen as 'one of the boys'. You have got to move away from that space. I was clear to every player that I coached, even the ones I had played with, that my role is to get the best out of you and that it will require me to challenge you at some stage and I am not shy to do that. They never tried to encourage me to be one of the boys. There was a lot of respect for that.

"If you think of the best batsman in the world, he scores over 50 in one in three innings. That is 33 per cent of the time making a score of 50. You can't expect more than that. Each player is different and manages that space differently. It would be our responsibility to help him get back in that form. Ultimately we have recruited him to the job because we think he is the best.

"But it is part and parcel of the game, dealing with failure. The older you get, the more experienced you are, the greater perspective you get on results.

"When we prepared for the World Cup 2011 with the Indian team, I can't remember one occasion where we spoke about winning the World Cup. We knew that if we did things right, we would get the best chance of success. So we spent less time worrying about the results and more time worrying about our processes."

Gary Kirsten
Born 23 November 1967
International career: 1993–2004

	M	Inns	NO	Runs	HS	Avg	SR	100	50	Conv
Tests	101	176	15	7 289	275	45.27	43	21	34	38.18
First-class	221	387	42	16 670	275	48.31	47*	46	79	36.80
ODIs	185	185	19	6 798	188*	40.95	72	13	45	22.41
List A	294	289	27	9 586	188*	36.58	71*	18	58	23.68

8

Jacques Kallis

"**I** think he's been a rock. He's proper. I haven't seen a better cricketer than Jacques Kallis."

Those are the words of Brian McMillan, himself a distinguished all-rounder, teammate of Jacques in the late 1990s and a shrewd analyst of the game. The legendary Australian captain Steve Waugh is unhesitating in his assessment of Kallis: "One of the greatest cricketers of all time."

Jacques played in 166 Tests – only three men have notched up more (Sachin Tendulkar, Ricky Ponting and Steve Waugh), and only Tendulkar has scored more centuries than Kallis. Of the 11 players who have made more than 10 000 Test runs, only the Sri Lankan Kumar Sangakkara has a better average, and then marginally: 58.04 to Kallis's 55.37. Only 14 batsmen in Test history have a higher batting average than Kallis.

In addition, Kallis is seventh on the all-time batting list in ODIs with 11 579 runs. In 103 of his 314 innings (33 per cent), he scored more than 50 or 100 – a ratio better than Tendulkar's (32 per cent) and Lara's (28 per cent). And in ODI matches, his average of 44.36 is bettered by only 11 of 73 men who have scored more than 5 000 runs.

Jacques says he has always been indifferent to statistics. When Ali pointed out that Jacques's first-class batting average ranked alongside those of Barry Richards and Graeme Pollock, he affirmed that he had never thought he might reach that level. "Definitely not," he said. "As a youngster you just want to do well so that you can retain your place early on, and help whatever team you are playing for to win games of cricket.

"I never looked at stats – that's probably one of the blessings that I had. I tried to just play according to the situation of the game. I certainly didn't start out my career trying to be the best player South Africa has produced. I played the game of cricket because I loved and enjoyed it. I've always believed that if you take care of the stuff on the field, off the field stuff takes care of itself. If you're producing the goods to win games of cricket, the stats come by themselves.

"I was more about being the best player that I could possibly be, rather than comparing myself to others. I can't control what others are doing. I can only control what I am doing."

Kallis made his Test debut in 1995, but Ali recalls that he really revealed a big-match temperament in his seventh Test at Melbourne in 1997, when he scored his maiden century.

"The Melbourne Cricket Ground holds 100 000 people, but it was pretty empty on the Monday," says Ali. "It was extraordinary, the acoustics – whatever the players said, you could hear it in the stands. I can see it as if it was yesterday: Michael Kasprowicz bowling to Jacques, loud-mouthing and verbalising him. But he never flinched. Eventually Kasprowicz bowled a bouncer, without effect, and verbalised him again – and eventually Kasprowicz said: 'Is this man fucking deaf?'"

Kallis's personal milestone in that match was also a vital team contribution. South Africa had been skittled out by McGrath and Warne for 136 in the first innings, and were set a victory target of 381. Going into the final day, they were 79 for one and not expected to survive, let alone win. But Kallis, who was on 40 overnight, batted for most of the next day, and in all for more than six hours, to help salvage a draw. *Wisden* said that South Africa "owed much to an upright 101 from Kallis, which featured many stylish drives – and an indifference to the sledging of the close fielders".

After 18 years, 166 Test matches and 45 centuries, Jacques is still inclined to say that his first Test century was also his best innings. "I remember Brian McMillan saying to me at Melbourne – 'You'll do well to better that.' That century still sticks out for me, in terms of my own career and what was happening in the match. My place in the side still wasn't solidified, and the conditions in Australia were difficult, Shane Warne was at his best. And my hundred helped save the Test match for us."

Jacques took longer than any other batsman to make his first Test double-century, in terms of innings and time. The elusive 200 finally came 15 years after his debut, against India at Centurion in December 2010. He slaughtered the bowlers in concert with Hashim Amla (140) and AB de Villiers (129) as South Africa amassed 620 for four declared. Jacques passed 100 in only 130 balls, and 200 at almost the same rate (267 balls). Neil Manthorp wrote that "the dressing-room balcony was a picture of riotous celebration" when the double-century appeared on the scoreboard.

The long delay had never worried Kallis. "If I had finished my career and not got a double-hundred, I would have been disappointed, but I wouldn't have lost any sleep. It wasn't as big an issue for me as the media made it out to be. But once I got the 200, and the ovation I got at Centurion Park ... well, the whole match came to a halt. I then realised it meant a lot to people in this country, and especially my teammates. Those few minutes will live with me for the rest of my life when it comes to remembering one particular innings."

Ali has been following cricket closely since 1960: "The batsmen I played against with the best techniques were Colin Cowdrey and Barry Richards. Then along came Jacques and his technique was probably the best I have ever seen. Head over the ball, full face of the bat, moving late, good on the front foot and back foot, playing bat and pad together – terrific. Steve Waugh once told me the Australians tried everything when bowling against Kallis and had analysed him from A to Z, and they couldn't find any flaws."

If a player has an excellent technique, he is unlikely to experience a long bad trot, or sequence of low scores. Did Jacques work hard at his technique? "I was very fortunate in that I had a good start to my career. My dad taught me the basics of batting from a young age, even though he had never really played the game. He had a philosophy he instilled in me: if you're behind the ball, you can control the ball. So I always try to get behind the ball, not play away from the ball. But I also had some really good coaches along the way – Keith Richardson at Wynberg Boys' High, Duncan Fletcher at Western Province, Bob Woolmer with the national team.

"Babies need to crawl before they can walk – I pretty much did my cricket like that, too. I tried to make sure I had a strong base, and then aimed to expand from that. I also wanted to keep it very simple. If you haven't a good technique, it's difficult to get out of a bad trot."

In grade seven in 1989, the 12-year-old Kallis was teased unmercifully for wearing a helmet, but he didn't care. "That took the fear of getting hurt out of me. From then on I just played, I just wanted to bat and bat. I've always preferred batting to bowling. I was pretty small at school and I couldn't hit the ball out of the ground, so I had to learn a good technique to survive and try to rotate the strike." He was known for hating to get out; and when he wasn't playing in a game, he was usually seen in the nets.

Jacques liked practising, but he was flexible about the intensity. "I knew how I felt and what I needed to do. I always kept pretty fit physically, I enjoyed the training. I did quite a lot of running. I had a back injury when I was younger, and I got a lot stronger from the gym work, which helped a lot especially from a bowling point of view. I did weights, but not heavy weights. Stretching was very important to keep supple, which helped me throughout my career in not being injured too often.

Jacques Kallis: South Africa's greatest cricketer, his batting feats may never be equalled; he was renowned for his immense powers of concentration

"From a cricketing point of view, I would go on 'feel'. If I went to the nets and hit 15 balls and I felt good, I would walk out. I was a big believer that if I was hitting the ball well, I would just hit myself out of form if I spent too long in the nets. There were days when I didn't feel I was hitting it well and I would spend more time in the nets. I was never one to hit balls for the sake of hitting balls. I would rather do less work at a higher intensity." In this respect Jacques's approach was very similar to that of Graeme Pollock.

Ali pointed out to Jacques that, off the field, he has always been courteous, amenable and engaging – but on the field, incredibly tough mentally. "The Aussies really tried to get at you," Ali said to him. "Where did the toughness come from?"

"I think it was part of me," was Kallis's answer. "It might have had something to do with losing my mom at a young age, where you learn to overcome difficulties. Also, going out to bat is not that important when you put it into perspective. There are people out there fighting and dying in wars, so am I really under that much pressure? I was very good at not over-complicating situations – that was my way of dealing with it. From a chirping point of view – there is a lot of it, but when the bowler runs in, there's silence. The words can't get you out. It's the ball that's going to get you out. I kind of enjoyed the chirping – it got me going. If I wasn't quite up to the challenge on a particular day, not 100 per cent there mentally, then the odd word from a fielder or an early bouncer or two inspired me. I never really reacted back. In life as well, I put things in perspective – I try to make things as simple as possible."

Kallis was known for his ability to "get into the zone": impervious to distraction, placid and undemonstrative. Typically, after he played a shot and there was no run, he immediately turned his back and walked a few yards. "In between balls, I think whatever I want to. I look around, look at the crowd. Then, when the bowler gets back to his mark, I switch on again and face the next ball. I've never believed that words get you out. It's the leather ball that gets you out.

I do hear what the fielders are saying, and sometimes I might have a chuckle under my breath, but it's never really affected me. I've worked at being mentally strong, and being able to switch off between balls. What they say can't take my focus off the next delivery."

Jacques's ability to focus relentlessly, along with his physical fitness and stamina, eventually translated into some of the most impressive statistics the game has seen.

In the 2003–04 season, he became one of only four men (Donald Bradman was the first, Kallis the second) to make a century in five successive Tests. He hit 158, 177 and 130 not out against the West Indies in South Africa, followed by two more unbeaten innings of 130 (again) and 150 in New Zealand.

In one of those Tests, in Hamilton in 2004, he hit 92 and then, wrote *Wisden*, "on a day that varied from engrossing to downright boring, Jacques Kallis displayed tremendous application to strike an unbeaten 150 on a deteriorating pitch. Neil McKenzie, who knocked a busy 52 in the morning, played the ideal Robin to Kallis's Batman … Kallis and McKenzie mixed caution with aggression to keep New Zealand's bowlers – particularly the spinners – at bay. All the while, Kallis revealed an array of shots as effective as his padwork. When the spinners pitched the ball on the scuffmarks, he stood back – often inches from the stumps – and played it as late as possible. But when they strayed, a damaging sweep shot often came into play. The faster bowlers provoked a different response. He cut repeatedly, and pushed the ball through the covers, and when Scott Styris bowled, the slower pace allowed Kallis the time and control to drive straight down the ground."

In two successive Test matches in Pakistan in 2007, he made 155, 100 not out, 59 and 107 not out to drive South Africa to a rare series win on the subcontinent. "Not content with the damage he caused with the bat," said *Wisden*, "Kallis took a stunning catch in the slips and chipped in with the ball", taking three wickets in the series for 80 runs. Pakistan must have been heartily sick of the sight of him. Six months earlier, in a three-Test series against them in South Africa, he had made 272 runs, including 60 not out, 91 and 51 (and had taken 10 wickets).

Kallis followed those three tons in Pakistan with 186 and 131 the next month, in November 2007, in two Tests at home against New Zealand – which meant he had scored five centuries in four successive Tests.

As Jacques's career progressed, his average rose steadily and so did his batting tempo. After 120 Tests, his average levelled out at around 56, but he raised his scoring rate further. This is especially impressive because the longer a man's career, the less impact is made statistically by later performances. He admits that "there were times when I could have dominated more. But for years I tried to bat through an innings. The side expected to bat around me. Then when our batting line-up became stronger, I had the opportunity to be more aggressive, especially in Test cricket – and I have scored faster in the past few years."

His conversion rate beyond 50 indicates his reliability and his value to his side. But his ratio of centuries-to-innings is, if anything, more impressive. Among his contemporaries from all countries who have played more than 50 Tests, Kallis's frequency of scoring centuries (in 16 per cent of his innings) is the equal highest with Sangakkara and Matthew Hayden, and in cricket history only Bradman (a freakish 36 per cent) and Herbert Sutcliffe (19 per cent) are better.

After his retirement from Tests and ODIs, Jacques continued to play T20 cricket. This format "has been unbelievable for the game of cricket," he says. "It has brought excitement back to the game, attracted a new audience. However, Test cricket is still the be-all and end-all. Again, it boils down to my belief that a baby crawls before it walks. I still think cricketers need to make sure they have that base, establish their technique first before they start trying to hit balls out of the park."

Like Gary Kirsten, Jacques believes that the 1999 World Cup "was the one that got away from us. All one-day cricket is about depth in batting. If you bat right down to 9 and 10, you can do very well. In a World Cup, it will happen that you're going to be 40 for four at some stage – especially in those conditions in England. You need to be able to recover, and that 1999 team had that capacity." That explains why the biggest disappointment of Jacques's career was the failure to win the 1999 World Cup. "You try to put things in perspective, but that was the closest as anything can be to feeling that someone had died. To go from such a high, thinking we were through – there were ebbs and flows, we were behind, then we were on top, going through so many emotions – and then we lost."

Jacques also has views on the choke factor: "Looking back at my career, if there was one thing I could have changed about the way we approached World Cups, I would have made sure we enjoyed them more than we did. The trouble was we changed the way we did things because it was a World Cup. That put us under unnecessary pressure, and by the time you get to the important games, you're exhausted."

Of all the Test sides Jacques played in, he believes the best was the one that beat both England and Australia away in 2008.

Who were the best bowlers he faced?

"Wasim Akram was the best I've faced – the one bowler that really stood out. He swung the ball both ways with the same action, and he had a nasty bouncer that was very difficult to pick up. And he had good pace. He could bowl with the new ball and then come back with the old ball and reverse-swing it. He was unbelievable at the death in one-day cricket. From the other end, Waqar could bowl big out-swingers with the new ball, and come back with the old ball with an in-swinger that would kill your toes."

Who was the best spinner he faced, Muralitharan or Warne? "It was Warne, without a doubt. Leg-spin is the toughest bowling art. To do it as long as he did, and as well as he did, is incredible – to land the ball so accurately, and hardly ever give you a bad ball. He could contain, and he could take wickets at will. He is a legend."

In looking to capture the amazing career of Jacques Kallis, the statistics don't lie but they also don't tell the full story. The greatness of Kallis does not ever seem to have been acknowledged emotionally by South African fans. Foreign commentators have also noticed this. Stephen Brenkley, writing in the *Independent* newspaper in 2012, said that "for most of the 17 years he has been on the international circuit, Kallis has been a formidable player but he has never been a fashionable one". The Indian commentator Harsha Bhogle argued that "Kallis is a connoisseur's cricketer rather than a seat-grabber. He is like the concrete that holds up a building rather than the laminate that gives it the gloss."

Can it have been that Kallis was less accessible and less emotional than some of his colleagues? Standing in the slips with his reflective sunglasses, he seemed inscrutable. It was said of him that he got "in the zone", which is another way of describing his powers of concentration – but that may also have produced an impression of coldness. Yet he certainly displayed smiles and emotion whenever he scored a century, and there is no doubt that he took visible pleasure in the success of the team.

Jacques Kallis is the greatest cricketer produced by South Africa, and perhaps its greatest batsman. The main rivals for that title, Graeme Pollock and Barry Richards, had abbreviated careers and did not have the chance to play in Test matches against all countries.

Jacques Kallis
Born 16 October 1975
International career: 1995–2013

	M	Inns	NO	Runs	HS	Avg	SR	100	50	Conv
Tests	166	280	40	13 289	224	55.37	46	45	58	43.68
First-class	257	421	57	19 695	224	54.10	47*	62	97	38.99
ODIs	328	314	53	11 579	139	44.36	73	17	86	16.50
List A	424	406	65	14 845	155*	43.53	73	23	109	17.42

PART FIVE

TRANSFORMATION, EXILE AND CAPTAINCY

9

Graeme Smith

South Africa produced some outstanding players after readmission to world cricket in 1991 and the national team was generally competitive against all opposition. However, at the start of the 2008 series in England, observers pointed out the stark fact that in 17 years since readmission, South Africa had won only two series against England or Australia in 14 attempts. And in 26 series against England since 1889, South Africa had achieved only two series wins out of 13 in England, in 1935 and 1965 – and none in eight series in Australia since the first encounter in 1902.

After the first innings of the first Test at Lord's in July 2008, it seemed that this frustratingly poor record was unlikely to change. England made a massive 593 for eight declared, including 152 in just 181 balls from Kevin Pietersen and 199 by Ian Bell. South Africa struggled to 247 all out and followed on. By the end of the third day, they were 13 without loss, needing another 333 just to make England bat again. To go one down in a four-match series would put a series win almost out of reach.

Then the two Old Edwardians, Graeme Smith and Neil McKenzie, made a stand of 204 for the first wicket – the highest ever opening partnership for South Africa in the second innings of a Test. At the end of the day, just 229 runs had been added and the England total was still 104 runs away – but only one wicket was down. Smith had taken five hours and 40 minutes on his 107.

Of this epic fourth day, Sambit Bal wrote: "Test cricket is all about context, and in the context of this match, and the series, it was a compelling day: slow, but always simmering; lacking in action, but not plot and intrigue. It was just the kind that makes watching Test cricket a varied, rich and rewarding experience. If South Africa manage to draw this Test, it will be counted among the greatest of escapes in the history of the game, and this seemingly dull day will be regarded as the one that made it possible." Of Smith's innings, Bal wrote that "the situation today demanded him to bat against his natural instincts and he tempered his game admirably. The product was an industrious hundred, and perhaps the most valuable of his career."

South Africa did indeed escape and draw the Test. The next day McKenzie took his total to 138, 31 runs more than Smith's innings but taking four hours longer. Hashim Amla supported McKenzie with 104, enabling a declaration at 393 for three. Bad light prevented further play in the match. It was only the second time in history that a team following on had produced three centuries.

After seeming so much in command, England had fielded for more than two days and their bowlers were exhausted for the second Test at Headingley, starting only a few days later. This time it was South Africa's turn to establish a first-innings lead of more than 300 as they piled up 522 (Smith 44, Prince 149, De Villiers 174), and they went on to win by 10 wickets. It was Smith's 28th victory as captain in 59 matches, moving past Hansie Cronje's record 27 wins in 53 Tests.

The third Test at Edgbaston produced one of the great matches in history. England made 231, South Africa made 314, and England replied with 363. Thanks to a scoring rate of well above three runs per over in each of the first three innings, when South Africa went out to bat just before lunch on the fourth day, they had plenty of time – a day and two sessions – to make the 281 runs needed to win.

In earlier eras, a South African side in such a position would have gone on the defensive, aiming to preserve wickets and hope that the runs would come. But it was a measure of the growing influence of Smith's captaincy style over the previous five years that he and McKenzie did not hang about. After lunch they put on 65 in just 75 minutes – and then four quick wickets were lost as McKenzie went for 22 and the heart of the top order – Amla, Jacques Kallis and Ashwell Prince – managed only 13 runs between them. Suddenly an England victory was in sight: 188 still needed by South Africa, and the sixth batsman already at the crease.

But De Villiers stayed 100 minutes with Smith and added just 27 in a partnership of 78 – then it was five wickets down, with 110 runs still needed. Mark Boucher came in and stayed for nearly two hours for 45 runs. By the time the victory target was reached, still with five wickets down, Smith had an unbeaten 154, made in five hours 40 minutes. Cricinfo described it as "one of the finest centuries in a run-chase … Smith wore a steely determination throughout his innings as he steadily lost partners and had to be at his very best to combat a wearing surface, which offered particular assistance to Monty Panesar from the footmarks. He played positively from the outset, but without being reckless."

Nobody before Smith had scored a century in the fourth innings of a Test at Edgbaston, and the winning score of 283 for five was the highest fourth-innings total at the ground.

England captain Michael Vaughan said afterwards: "I am more gutted than anyone because I fully expected us to win today. It's the first time I have ever lost back-to-back games, and certainly midway through the day I expected us to bowl them out for 200 and win quite comfortably. But we've just witnessed a very special innings from Graeme Smith, and he deserves all the plaudits he's going to get."

Smith himself regards that unbeaten 154 as his most meaningful Test innings. However, "that morning I didn't want to get out of bed," he remembered. "The game was carefully poised, there was huge pressure, and I had no breakfast. I caught the team bus just one minute before it left for the ground. Before lunch I had six overs to face and my batting was horrendous. But after lunch everything just fell into place – and that was probably my best Test knock."

South Africa were now 2-0 up with one to play: their first series win against England in 43 years. The fourth Test at the Oval was inevitably an anti-climax. Smith made 46 and 0 and England won by six wickets.

With a settled, experienced and confident South African side, the timing of the 2008–09 series in Australia could not have been better. At this stage of his career, Smith had made 16 Test centuries, and his 5761 runs had been made at a strike rate of 61 per 100 balls – the next highest was De Villiers at 53. Smith had proved himself not only as a formidable accumulator of runs, but as one of the fastest scorers in Test cricket – which was crucial in creating the space for his bowlers to take wickets.

On Smith's previous visit to Australia as captain in 2005–06, he had not led from the front as a batsman: only 155 runs in six Test innings, with a top score of 39. Peter Roebuck noted that he came across as loud and brash, "looking for trouble, seeking confrontation, trying to show that he was not afraid. He could not match his words with deeds. As a consequence he was taken apart."

In 2008, however, Smith said little in advance of the Tests, and under his leadership the team had gathered much self-confidence, collectively and individually.

The first Test in Perth in December 2008 produced a spellbinding, lurching, entirely unpredictable contest – and the second biggest successful run-chase in Test history.

Australia batted first and posted 375 at the rate of 3.79 runs per over – but only after recovering from being 15 for three at one stage. South Africa were demolished by Mitchell Johnson (eight for 61, including a spell of five for two in 21 balls) and managed only 281, and Australia then made 319. The lowest run rate for

Graeme Smith: one of the great captains from all countries, with a capacity for really big scoring and a reputation for imposing his will on the opposition

the three innings was 3.12 per over, but no batsman found it easy – neither side produced a century and there were only six fifties.

South Africa needed 414 to win, and again, said *Wisden*, "Smith led from the front, putting his aching elbow out of mind to strike 13 bruising fours, pass 6,000 career runs and complete his sixth Test century (108) of the year". The statisticians also noted that Smith's century was his third in the fourth innings of a match, each time leading to victory.

The job wasn't done when Smith was out, but with the score on 172 for two, at 3.44 runs per over, the foundation had certainly been laid. There were three century partnerships in the innings as Amla (53), De Villiers (106 not out) and JP Duminy (50 not out) steered the side to a six-wicket win that was widely described as the finest of the post-apartheid era – better even than the thriller at Sydney in 1994. Ali said at the time: "I believe this to be our best Test win ever. Surely our finest moment … it's an extraordinary performance."

In the second Test in Melbourne in January 2009, Australia again batted first and again compiled an imposing total of 394. Despite a solid 62 from Smith, South Africa's top order came and went; the score slipped to 184 with only three wickets left, and the follow-on was a possibility. But JP Duminy, coming in at number six, kept going with the unexpected help of two specialist bowlers, Paul Harris and Dale Steyn.

At the end of the second day, South Africa were on 198 for seven (Duminy 35, Harris 8), trailing by 196 runs. By the end of the next day, amazingly, they were leading by 65 runs. Harris (39) batted for more than an hour, and then Duminy (166) and Steyn (76) stayed together for four hours and 382 balls, while adding 189 runs – the third highest ninth-wicket stand in history. Australia's confidence was shattered (Steyn followed up his record Test score with five wickets for 67, ten for 154 in the match), and South Africa were set a winning target of 183 with more than a day to get it.

Smith again led the way, with 75 in 94 balls, as South Africa won by nine wickets. Commentator Neil Manthorp wrote that, having devoured every delivery of the Perth Test match, "I fully expected to wait another 20 years to see something so special. Instead, it came a week later at Melbourne."

Smith's 137 runs in the match took his total for the calendar year to 1 656 at an average of 72 – only two men had ever scored more in a year. Barry Richards said Smith had shown "a lot of maturity as a skipper, and as a player he really has come to the fore. He has led by example and he has kept a cool head all the way through."

The significance of the win went beyond the field of play. "When Hashim Amla flicked another ball off his pads and scampered the winning run," noted Peter Roebuck, "he achieved more than a mere victory. It was a stroke that spoke for generations of Indian crick-eters unable to compete for places in the national team. Suddenly they knew their records meant something, that they had been right, the champions of previous generations could play the game. When JP Duminy constructed his accomplished innings, he was representing a coloured community that languished for so many years in a twilight world. When Makhaya Ntini took wickets, he was uplifting downtrodden tribes."

No previous South African team had won a series in Australia, and no country had ever beaten both England and Australia in the space of seven months. It was Australia's first home series defeat in 16 years.

Smith played another dramatic role in the third Test in Sydney. South Africa needed 376 in their second innings to win, and at 190 for seven when De Villiers went out, the cause looked hopeless. But the fast bowlers Steyn and Ntini put on 55 runs for the 9th wicket. When Steyn was out for 28, a win was out of the question. A draw was now possible, though, because the partnership had used up 90 minutes – but nine wickets were down and it was not clear whether Smith would bat.

Smith had retired hurt with 30 in the first innings, his hand broken by Mitchell Johnson. His elbow had already been in chronic pain, and he did not expect to play again in the match. That was why, said *Wisden*, "he arrived in the morning without any gear. But when he decided he was needed, he found some pants in his cricket bag protecting his bats. A shirt was borrowed from Jacques Kallis and Paul Harris's pullover was worn with a hamburger stain on it. He took off the plastic cast that had been protecting the fifth finger on his left hand and a re-modelled glove was put on instead. There were no painkillers, and he was unable to dress himself. Morné Morkel laced up Smith's spikes. Even before his finger injury, simple tasks such as brushing his teeth were too painful. He started to pad up when Ntini went out to bat, and the target had shrunk to 50 deliveries when he took guard."

With the series won and this match beyond winning, nobody would have criticised Smith for not coming in to bat. Yet he did, producing a mini-drama no less engrossing than the most exciting periods of the previous two Tests. Needing to survive for eight overs and two balls, he was bowled by Johnson with just five minutes and ten balls remaining.

"History in the making," Ali called it, after the series. "How good is the South African team? Certainly after our return to international cricket, the two best teams we had in Test cricket was the one led by the late Hansie Cronje in the late 1990s and this current one. But the records will show this team is better. They started by beating Pakistan in Pakistan, beat England in England, drew with India in India and now they have beaten Australia in Australia – there can be no question they are number one in world cricket today."

It was the start of a golden era in Tests for South Africa. Four years later, Smith captained South Africa to a similar series Test double over England and Australia, with the core of the team unchanged – four all-time great batsmen in Smith, Kallis, Amla and De Villiers, and Steyn and Morkel the fast bowlers.

At the start of the 2012 series in England, the home side were rated the best in the world. They batted first in the opening Test at the Oval and made 385. No side would expect to lose by an innings after posting such a total, but that is what happened. South Africa replied with an astonishing 637 for two (Smith 131 in six hours, Amla 311 not out, Kallis 182 not out) and then Steyn took five for 57 as England made 240 in the second innings to lose by an innings and 12 runs.

Wisden noted that "the left-handed Smith was initially unsettled by (spinner) Graeme Swann, so he eschewed all risk by lunging defensively forward or playing from the crease – a viable option against such sluggish turn. The result was a fifty high on determination and low on aesthetics; at 160 balls, it was his slowest in Tests. (His next fifty, though, came from just 41, as he became the seventh player to mark his 100th Test with a century.) Session merged into session as milestone after milestone slipped by under increasingly blue skies."

Gary Kirsten, by then the coach of South Africa, commented after the match: "We've got some real class in our batting line-up. We've got guys with a lot of experience and guys who enjoy batting a lot. They don't give their wickets away. They take pride in spending a lot of time at the crease. It was particularly satisfying as a coach to see that."

The second Test was a high-scoring draw, with Smith making 52 in each innings. In the third and final match at Lord's, the sides were separated by only six runs on the first innings. The only century of the match on either side came from Amla, and South Africa won by 51 runs. The series was won 2-0, and after the match Smith received the mace for the team rated number one in Test cricket – "the greatest triumph of his formidable reign".

South Africa's next Test match came three months later in Brisbane, which produced a high-scoring draw. The second Test in Adelaide was also drawn – but only after some extraordinary fighting cricket. "In pitiless heat," wrote Gideon Haigh, "and at a ground in the throes of extensive rebuilding, South Africa staged a four-day retreat after a disastrous start, and had just enough in reserve to keep the series at 0-0."

Australia started with 550 at a scorching rate of 5.12 per over. South Africa replied with 388 at 3.11 an over; Smith batted for nearly five hours for 122. Australia then set South Africa 430 to win. For once Smith failed with a duck, and without his steadiness his side collapsed to 134 for five. Then Faf du Plessis, who had made 78 in the first innings on debut, made 110 not out in seven hours and 45 minutes, batting throughout the last day and supported mainly by De Villiers (33) and Kallis (46), who was batting with a pulled hamstring.

Until the last over an Australian victory remained possible: "The tail provided further passive resistance, as Siddle hurled himself into the fray during a last, puffing, panting, red-faced, valiant spell, yorking Kleinveldt with four overs to go and two wickets required. But the game ended with Morkel blocking out the last over."

"South Africa now demonstrated that their number one Test ranking was a function not only of winning, but of not losing too," said *Wisden*. "At first it appeared that batsmen operating so defensively must eventually err through negativity, but the pitch was now playing truly: the challenge was concentration and endurance rather than deceitful deliveries. The pair batted deep into the day, before De Villiers finally nicked the second new ball from Siddle after an innings of 220 deliveries, from only 23 of which he scored; he did not hit a single boundary."

The English commentator Mark Nicholas wrote how Du Plessis, "in mainly 34 degrees of heat and high humidity, with five different partners, one of whom could barely run, defied a voracious Australian attack and saved a crucial match for his beloved country. This was a monumental effort, performed on debut and already written into the folklore of South African cricket."

In the third Test in Perth, Australia had to select a new pace attack after the bowlers had exhausted themselves at Adelaide. Du Plessis top-scored with 78 as his side took a first innings lead of 52 – and then the South African batsmen ran wild in the second innings. After Smith provided yet another vital foundation with 84 in just 100 balls, there were big centuries for Amla and De Villiers in a total of 569. Australia fell short of the winning target of 632 by 310 runs – this innings defeat was the biggest ever for Australia against South Africa. Of their second innings, Australian captain Ricky Ponting said: "That was them trying to impose themselves on the series, and they did it better than I have seen any team take a game away from the opposition before. A lot of the other teams we have played over the years who have been in that position have been too scared to do that."

After the third Test and the 1-0 series win, Ali called Graeme Smith's team "the most successful South African side of all time". Apart from the series wins, the other statistics supported this view. Dale Steyn is possibly the best fast bowler ever produced by this country, and Jacques Kallis is the best all-rounder in history after Sobers. At that time we had four of the top seven batsmen in the world rankings – Amla (2), Kallis (4), De Villiers (5) and Smith (7) – and the top two bowlers, Steyn and Vernon Philander.

David wrote in his column in the *Financial Mail* after the series that "the 1970 four-test thrashing of Australia by Ali Bacher's side continues to give satisfaction to those who remember it. They grow misty-eyed in particular over the second test in February in Durban, where the Springboks (as they then were) won by an innings and 129 runs, after posting a record 622 for nine declared. In particular, the old-timers single out the sparkling 103-run partnership between Barry Richards and Graeme Pollock in just an hour after lunch.

"But how quickly was that 622 made? Although they finished the first day at 386 for five, it comes as a surprise to find that the Springbok run rate for the completed innings was 3.7 per over. That was quick for the time, but it was pedestrian compared to the scoring in SA's second innings in the third Test last weekend in Perth: 569 runs at a rate of 5.08 per over.

"As for the individual batsmen, Graeme Pollock is rightly remembered for his magnificent 274, then the highest Test score by a South African. But his strike rate (runs per 100 balls faced) was 68. Barry Richards nearly achieved the rare distinction of a century before lunch on the first day of a Test (he was 94 not out) and finished on 140 at a strike rate of 85.

"But that 140 was scored only marginally faster than Graeme Smith's 84 in 100 balls last weekend – and they were both slower than Hashim Amla (196 runs at a strike rate of 88) and AB de Villiers (169 at 91, not far off a run a ball).

"The brilliant 309-run victory on Monday gave SA the series – the second successive away win over Australia – and confirmed us as the top team in the world. But until Smith and Amla switched over to the offensive after tea on the second day, you could have argued that Australia were ahead in the series (to use a boxing analogy) on points.

"We had to battle to salvage a draw in Brisbane, and in Adelaide it was only the heroics of Faf du Plessis, who batted all day in the second innings, that saved us from a crushing defeat.

"Just after tea on Saturday in Perth, we were 28 for one. Amla and Smith then blasted 173 runs in just over 25 overs. This was against an attack that had reduced us to 75 for six in the first innings. By the end of Saturday the Australian morale was shattered.

"Not even the legends of 1970 could have played with more crowd-pleasing aggression, ruthlessness and courage."

As Smith pointed out, "there are people in our set-up that have taken many beatings at the hands of Australia. We know what is required to come here and be victorious. When we get on the plane, I will have a warm feeling to have been a part of something incredible and something special, and to have been able to share with guys who have put in an immense amount of hard work behind the scenes to celebrate these moments.

"I am extremely proud to be a part of the last nine matches. For us to win back-to-back Test series in England and Australia is an immense effort. You just have to look back and see how long it took us to get here. Now to be able to take that and play in front of our home fans will be great."

It was not only on the field that Smith's captaincy impressed. Ponting had announced that the Perth Test would be his last, and he was both surprised and delighted by the guard of honour that Smith ordered for him when he left the field at the end of play. "Graeme's gesture and the South African team's gesture, that sort of stuff will remain with me for ever, and I told him that on the field today." "Having played against Ricky so much over the years," Smith replied, "he's certainly the player I respect most."

Smith deserved to savour his second series win in Australia, a few months short of a decade after he had been made captain of South Africa at the age of just 22.

Ali had heard of his potential a few years before that appointment: "The late Bob Woolmer contacted me to tell me about a new young opening batsman. His name was Graeme Smith, and Bob told me that he was going to be even better than Gary Kirsten. Even though Bob was a good judge of talent, this was a bold prediction to make. Kirsten was by then a rock at the top of the South African order, a left-hander who had accumulated over 7 000 Test runs with 21 centuries, a highest score of 275 and a batting average in excess of 45.

"Now a new left-handed opener named Smith had made his bow in provincial cricket and people were saying good things about him. As it turned out, we had attended the same school, King Edward VII in Johannesburg, but I had yet to meet him."

Smith had attended Risidale Primary School in Johannesburg, where he "loved all sports" and was selected for provincial soccer and athletics. He was especially keen on cricket, though, and was offered bursaries to attend St Stithians and Michaelhouse, two of South Africa's leading private boys' schools. Although his father was a Jeppe old boy, Graeme wanted to go to their great rivals King Edward's, a leading public school.

At high school Smith always played one year above his age group, and when he was 14 he played adult club cricket for the Old Edwardian 1st XI. He matriculated from King Edward's in 1999, after three years in the 1st XI and captaining the side in his last two years. His potential was evident at the start of his high school career: the school magazine said of his performance in the Under-14A team that "he looked to be a most capable batsman and his aggregate of 349 runs at an average of 43 was a really good effort". At the end of 1998, his second year in the 1st XI, he was picked for the South African Schools and SA Under-19 sides. "He demonstrated his class," noted the magazine of that year. "His thoroughly professional approach enabled him to continue his astonishing sequence of scores both when on song or out of sorts – his determination to succeed was an example to all." His scores that season included unbeaten innings of 101 against Durban High School and 102 against Jeppe, and other centuries against St John's and Randburg.

Smith made his first-class debut in the 1999–2000 season, scoring 187 for a UCB Invitation XI against Griqualand West. Over the next two seasons he scored more than 1 500 runs, including four centuries and five fifties. In March 2002 he was picked for South Africa in the second Test against Australia at Newlands. He went in at number three and made just three in nine balls before being caught by Ricky Ponting off the bowling of Brett Lee.

This was arguably one of the two or three strongest Australian sides in history, with a bowling attack of Lee, Glenn McGrath, Shane Warne (playing in his 100th Test) and Jason Gillespie. However, in the second innings, Smith did enough to reassure the selectors by making 68 in three hours and 40 minutes. His next 10 Test innings included scores of 42, 200, 73 and 151. The double-hundred was against a weak Bangladesh attack, but the 151 came in a first-wicket partnership of 368 with Herschelle Gibbs, against Pakistan at Newlands – a South African Test record for any wicket at the time.

Smith also made his one-day international debut in March 2002, and a year later played in his 22nd ODI, making 35 in the disastrous World Cup quarter-final in Durban against Sri Lanka. The miscalculation of the runs needed by South Africa to win the match meant exit from the competition and the dismissal of Shaun Pollock as national captain.

Ali takes up the story: "With only eight Tests under his belt, Graeme was appointed national captain in March 2003 at the age of 22 – South Africa's youngest ever captain. I was 21 when I first captained Transvaal and 28 when appointed captain of South Africa. I therefore had seven years of tough provincial captaincy experience under my belt in hard, competitive cricket against such rival skippers as Jackie McGlew, who was the best captain I ever played against. But to be cast into the national captaincy at the age of 22 after just eight Test matches was quite unique and presented young Graeme with a huge challenge.

"Immediately after his appointment, he asked to meet me. I was then the executive director of the ICC Cricket World Cup and he came to our offices at Summer Place in Sandton. He was neatly dressed in his blazer and tie, and made an immediate impression on me. We spent almost an hour together. Two things impressed me – firstly, the pride and passion that he expressed in playing for and being asked to captain South Africa; and secondly his expressed desire to restore honesty and integrity to the game in the wake of the King Commission into match-fixing that was still fresh in our memories. So I have been supportive of him from day one – and he knows that.

"I can remember phoning Omar Henry, who was chairman of

the selection panel that appointed Graeme. I complimented him on the courage and vision that was required in taking such a bold decision with the future in mind."

Smith had a quiet start in the captaincy with two Tests against Bangladesh, and then came his astonishing, record-breaking feats in England in 2003. The force of his batting and of his personality crushed English morale and forced their captain, Nasser Hussain, into retirement after one Test in the series – after he had rashly said South Africa were "there for the taking".

In the first Test at Edgbaston in July 2003, Smith accumulated a massive 277, breaking the South African individual record of 275 held by Gary Kirsten and Daryll Cullinan. With Herschelle Gibbs (179) he put on 338 for the first wicket, the best opening partnership ever against England. It was also the second 300+ partnership for Smith and Gibbs, a feat matched in all Tests by only one other pair, Australia's Don Bradman and Bill Ponsford against England in 1934.

Smith declared the first innings at 594 for five, scored at more than four runs an over. He had become the youngest captain to score a Test century. Though the game ended in a draw, Smith added another 85 runs in the second innings; his match aggregate of 362 passed the South African record of 309 by Bruce Mitchell at the Oval in 1947.

At Lord's in the second Test, Makhaya Ntini took five for 75 as England crashed to 173 all out – and Smith picked up where he had left off. After being dropped (by Hussain) when he had eight, he hit 259, starting with a 133-run partnership with Gibbs; then 257 for the second wicket with Kirsten; then 123 with Boeta Dippenaar. Smith was able to declare on 682 for six (which remains the record total for South Africa) and even though England responded with 408, they had been facing their biggest ever first-innings deficit of 509: they lost by an innings and 92 runs, with Ntini taking 10 wickets in the match.

Smith had 621 runs in two successive Tests – only Don Bradman (625 against England in 1934) and Graham Gooch (640 against New Zealand and India in 1990) had done better. Smith's 259 at Lord's remains the highest score by a foreign player at the ground, breaking the record set by Bradman's 254. "It was a remarkable achievement for one so young and carrying the added burden of the captaincy," says Ali.

Smith reached 500 for the series only eight days after it had started. His overall strike rate in three innings was 76 runs per 100 balls, a key factor in giving his bowlers time to attack and get England out. By way of comparison, Graeme Pollock's strike rate was 68/100 when he made 274 against Australia in Durban. The Springboks made 622 runs in that innings in 1970 at a rate of 3.7 per over; the Proteas at Lord's in 2003 scored at 3.85 per over.

Smith could not maintain his dominance: his scores in the remaining three Tests of 2003 were 35, 5, 2, 14, 18 and 19. South Africa did win at Leeds, but England won at both Nottingham and the Oval to square the series. As *Wisden* remarked, South Africa "were denied the spoils of a series that appeared to have been in their pockets".

In the series against the West Indies in the 2003–04 summer in South Africa, Smith and Gibbs put on 301 runs for the first wicket in the fourth and final Test at Centurion – thus recording their third 300+ opening partnership, a world record.

Smith made four centuries in his next 21 Tests – modest by his earlier standards – and his next bout of heavy scoring came only in the West Indies in April 2005, with scores of 148, 104, 126 and 50 not out in three successive Tests. But this series was followed by another slump in the 2005–06 season: six Tests against Australia, three home and three away, and three against New Zealand. In 17 innings that summer he made just 450 runs (including two fifties) at an average of 26.

Along the way, of course, there was a relentless programme of one-day internationals, generally blurring into each other and not lingering in the memory. But one match stood out. Played in Johannesburg on 12 March 2006, as part of a five-match series against Australia, it was to become known as the greatest ODI in history.

"It was a Sunday," Ali remembers, "and I was returning on a flight from Melbourne, having made a speech at the Commonwealth Games. Halfway through the flight the pilot made a sudden announcement: 'I have an update for you from the Wanderers stadium. The Aussies have just concluded their 50 overs and their final total stands at 434 for four!' I can recall turning to an Aussie sitting next to me and saying, 'Your pilot has a great sense of humour...'"

The Australians did indeed score 434 and there were few, if any, in the packed Wanderers who believed South Africa could possibly match them. During the break between innings, the stars of the hit movie *Tsotsi* paraded around the perimeter with their recently awarded Oscar for Best Foreign Film. This, it seemed, would have to be the consolation highlight of day. Some spectators decided not to watch the inevitable defeat and left early.

Graeme Smith had other ideas. He recalls feeling "shattered" at the carnage of the last 10 overs of the Australian innings, when 133 runs were conceded. In the dressing-room at the break, all was silent until Jacques Kallis said: "I think we have done well! The Australians are probably 15 runs short." That broke the tension. Coach Mickey Arthur worked out targets for the batsmen – "and everybody started laughing," says Smith.

Smith lost his opening partner Boeta Dippenaar early in the innings for 0. Smith then led from the front as he so often did, smashing 90 off 55 balls to keep South Africa in the game. Herschelle Gibbs then went on to play the innings of his life, hitting 175 in 111 balls. "It was at the 30-over mark, with the score on 279 for two, that we realised that victory was actually in our grasp," says Smith.

When Gibbs went out, "he remained in the toilet until victory was achieved". Smith himself could not watch at the end when Makhaya Ntini came to the crease with two runs wanted, one wicket left and three balls remaining. South Africa got the runs with one ball to spare – it was a famous victory, and those spectators who had gone home early cursed themselves for not keeping the faith.

However, Smith regards his best ODI innings as the unbeaten 134 not out he made in Kolkata in November 2005 against India, when he opened the batting with Andrew Hall. South Africa beat India by 10 wickets that day, and Smith vividly remembers 90 000 Indians starting to applaud them as they approached victory.

Before the 2008 Test series against England, Smith had played in 66 Test matches, scored 5 392 runs at an average of 48.57, with 14 centuries and 22 fifties. If he had retired then, his career would have been regarded as outstanding – but as a Test captain his best was yet to come, as we have seen above, starting with the dual series wins in England and Australia in 2008–09 and again in 2012–13.

In an article written in 2012, Ali reviewed Smith's decade in the national team, most of it as captain:

"Call it youthful inexperience, but there have been times in the past when Graeme has made some ill-considered or silly statements. Given that he was still young and learning his trade, this is forgivable. Also, there were perceptions that he was sometimes arrogant. I remember once talking at a Rotary dinner in Benoni and, when I mentioned his name, I was mortified to hear some of the audience booing.

"It is therefore heartening to state now that we have an international cricket captain who has matured immensely. Looking back, perhaps his only recent regret is that he did not pay sufficient tribute to Ricky Ponting for the role that Australia played in that greatest of all one-day games at the Wanderers when South Africa scored 438 runs to win.

"I believe that tactically he has become a very good captain – as good as this country has produced. Indeed, in the next few years he could well become the best we've ever had.

"Importantly, he leads from the front and therefore has the full support of his team. What I like about him is that on those occasions when South Africa have been asked to chase, say, 225 to win, he has not taken the cautious approach of teams gone by, but has adopted an aggressive attitude that regularly sees around 28 runs scored in the first four overs.

"Also, the courage he showed in going out to bat with a broken hand at Sydney earlier this year told of his commitment and won the hearts of people who might once have doubted him.

"His current Test batting average of 50.57 is better than any South African opener that has gone before. We always used Bruce Mitchell as the benchmark for opening batsmen, and his average was 48.88. In limited-overs cricket, Graeme also averages above 40. Mentally, he is very tough.

"As an on-side player, they don't come any better. He occasionally plays across the line – but so did Bradman – and he obviously has a very good eye.

"The fact that South African cricket is currently on a high has a lot to do with the contributions of Graeme Smith. I would just like to see him and his team doing more to promote cricket at grassroots level, at both the disadvantaged and advantaged levels, notwithstanding their onerous cricket commitments."

Firdose Moonda of Cricinfo described the exit in the 2011 World Cup as "an almighty choke" which gave Smith "his darkest day" as captain. He resigned the ODI captaincy, and attracted much criticism for not flying home with his team, travelling instead to Ireland to be with his wife-to-be and her family. "The 2011 World Cup was the toughest time in my career," he admits. "My own self-esteem and self-confidence really took a whack. I was trying to figure out if I was really the right person to try to take the team forward."

Graeme Smith's technique as a batsman looked awkward and ungainly to some, but it was undeniably effective. He took part in no fewer than seven Test opening partnerships in excess of 200 runs. These included the world-record 415 with Neil McKenzie against Bangladesh, and three 300+ partnerships with Herschelle Gibbs.

Ali regards him as "unquestionably the strongest on-side player I've ever seen. At times he would seem unbalanced, and he often played across the line. In all my years in cricket I cannot recall any international batsman receiving as much comment and even criticism about his faulty technique as Graeme has."

Peter Roebuck said before the tour to England in 2008, reflecting on Smith's unorthodoxy: "By and large it is considered unwise to deflect straight balls towards square leg. Always it prompts cries of exasperation from properly raised bowlers. Mozart might as well be played on an electric guitar. Before reading their first *Wisden*, budding batsmen are told that it is not the sort of shot played by respectable folk, or by those seeking a lengthy stint at the popping crease."

But, as Ali pointed out, Smith had "a phenomenal eye, enabling him to routinely hit good-length balls on the middle stump to mid-wicket. Something like 75 per cent of his scoring shots were on the leg side. This was because he had a 'closed' grip, not unlike the grip used to great effect by Don Bradman."

Smith acknowledges his debt to former Transvaal and South Africa opening batsman Jimmy Cook, who was and is still a regular coach at King Edward VII School. "He taught me to think like an opening bat, and taught me the fundamentals of opening the batting."

"I have never seen a kid so focused," Cook told Ali. "Graeme would concentrate for one and a half hours at a time in the nets and not communicate with the other boys. When he was 16, I told the Gauteng Cricket Board he would open for South Africa."

On technique, Cook said he tried to change Smith's preference for a strong bottom hand, but ultimately left it alone. At Western Province, Duncan Fletcher also tried to change his technique, but Smith reverted to the closed grip. Cook's only "strong advice" was that if Smith played late, he would minimise the risks of playing across the line of the ball. "He batted well when he played late, with good head position and balance. He was really only worried by left-armers bowling over the wicket." It is not surprising, then, that the Australian left-arm bowler Mitchell Johnson claimed Smith's wicket more than anyone else in Tests (nine times).

Smith rates Glenn McGrath as the best fast bowler he faced – "he was always one step ahead of the batsman". He hated facing the Pakistani Shoaib Akhtar – "with his long run-up and long hair, you couldn't see the ball at the point of delivery because of his slinging action". Others who impressed him were Australians Brett Lee and Jason Gillespie, and the Englishman Andrew Flintoff – "a difficult bowler when he came around the wicket to the left-hander". The best spin bowler he faced was Shane Warne – "a great competitor".

Mental toughness was needed against such bowlers, and, says Ali, "like Australians, mentally Graeme was very tough. In his first Test at Newlands, the Aussies sledged him without a break, but he ignored them and made a good fifty in the second innings. He also had the courage to score quickly. Like Eddie Barlow, who also opened for South Africa, he would usually score about 30 in the first four or five overs. That helps a side to seize the initiative and it puts uncertainty into the minds of the bowlers and the fielding captain."

Smith says his mindset "was always to be positive, to put pressure on the bowlers, even through my body language". At 6′4″, he aimed to use his body to let the bowler know he "was present at the wicket". The key for him was to hit the ball hard and as late as possible. He understood that he needed to play to his strengths – "I knew what I could do and not do."

Smith says he was always interested in leadership. At the age of 11 he recorded in writing that he wanted to captain South Africa. When he was appointed national captain, he says he was excited – "but I was too young to understand the job. Eric Simons asked me if I knew what I was in for. Shaun Pollock had phoned me after he was fired by the selectors after the 2003 World Cup, and he told me they were going to offer me the job – and that I must take it. The senior players were very supportive from the outset – Herschelle Gibbs, Jacques Kallis and Mark Boucher all phoned after the announcement to pledge their support."

Graeme Smith was the third-youngest Test captain in history when he was appointed at 22 years and 82 days. Peter Roebuck said that he got the job "because he looked captaincy material, lofty and fearless, and had a certain presence about him, besides which he was vigorous and ambitious, had not been worn down by politics, and seemed to be worth his place in a reconstructed side".

In the first part of his captaincy, says Smith, he had "a huge determination to succeed and a great passion for the job. I wanted to convey a sense of powerful influence, and so in some quarters I was seen as arrogant. I also wanted to lead from the front, which I was able to do. Those two double-tons in England in 2003 defined my career, and gave me time to grow. Otherwise I would not have lasted as captain."

After the 2007 World Cup, Smith began working with Paddy Upton, and he regards that as a turning point in his captaincy. "I now had a clear idea of what was required of a leader, and how to get the best out of my players," he said.

Jimmy Cook found Smith brash and arrogant as a captain at first – "he had to be to survive" – but thought he mellowed in later years. In fact, apart from school, he had very little captaincy experience before he became national captain: only three one-day games for South Africa 'A' against Zimbabwe. He now has the world record for Tests played as captain (109), with Allan Border (93) the next highest. Only one other captain from any country has won successive series in Australia: the Englishman Arthur Shrewsbury in the 19th century.

Gary Kirsten, who played his last Test series under Smith as captain and later coached the Proteas, told Cricinfo that Smith was the "greatest captain ever" in Test cricket. "I don't think anyone has led as long. We know that. He has taken South Africa to great heights. The kind of success he has had, the kind of success he has taken South African cricket to, I would argue that he is the best captain that has ever lived. For Graeme to end up with an average above 48, and then to have the type of leadership success he did have, is absolutely a massive achievement. You look at his record in the fourth innings and his ability to make important contributions. That gave the team a lot of confidence. It gives your team a lot of comfort to know that the captain is walking the talk."

Graeme Smith
Born 1 February 1981
International career: 2002–2014

	M	Inns	NO	Runs	HS	Avg	SR	100	50	Conv
Tests	117	205	13	9 265	277	48.25	60	27	38	41.53
First-class	165	284	19	12 916	311	48.73	59	37	51	42.04
ODIs	197	194	10	6 989	141	37.98	81	10	47	17.54
List A	259	253	15	9 331	141	39.20	80	14	67	17.28

10

Kevin Pietersen

Like Graeme Smith, Kevin Pietersen was a talented player at one of South Africa's leading state boys' schools and cricket nurseries (King Edward VII School and Maritzburg College respectively), who went on to play more than a hundred Tests and to captain his country – except that Pietersen played for England.

Like Tony Greig, Allan Lamb and Robin Smith before him, he was born, grew up and learned his cricket in South Africa and then claimed qualification for England through parentage (Pietersen's mother was English-born). But the other three players departed to represent England because they were denied the opportunity to play for South Africa in the apartheid era.

Pietersen, playing in the post-apartheid era, decided to move for a different political reason. He felt there would not be an opportunity for him to play for the Proteas because he would be disadvantaged by affirmative action. In his first book, *Crossing the Boundary*, he wrote: "I was dropped from the Natal side because the quota system was brought into South African cricket to positively discriminate in favour of 'players of colour' and to fast-track the racial integration of cricket in the country. To me, every single person in this world needs to be treated exactly the same and that should have included me, as a promising 20-year-old cricketer. If you do well you should play on merit. That goes for any person of any colour. It was heartbreaking. Even though it was very hard for me to take in at the time, it turned out it was the best thing that could have happened."

Shaun Pollock accompanied Pietersen and his father to see Ali, who was then CEO of the United Cricket Board of SA. "He was rude to me in that meeting and he was rude to my dad," said Pietersen in his book. "I had never met the man before. As far as I was concerned the least he could do was be polite. As soon as we left the meeting my dad said to me: 'You're going ... the quota system will never finish.'"

Ali does not recall much detail of the encounter – "but I know he was critical of how I handled that meeting. The way I recall it, he was disillusioned about South African cricket. His father, to put it bluntly, seemed to see no future for whites in South Africa, and he was pushing that his son should leave South Africa. I listened to Kevin's concern that he didn't have a permanent position in the Natal team, and he was angry at being dropped for a player, Goolam Bodi, whom he thought wasn't good enough. I said it's not a problem – we're short of quality spin bowlers in South Africa, because our cricket has been dominated by fast bowlers. I said that one phone call to Bloemfontein or Port Elizabeth, and I should be able to fix him up with a permanent spinners' place in a provincial team. That's about all I recall of the meeting."

Is there still bad blood between them? "Last year I read that he was coming out to South Africa for a two-day, six-a-side tournament at Old Edwardians," says Ali. "My nephew Adam was also involved in the tournament, as an Old Ed who'd played for the Proteas. I said to Adam that we didn't need to ask Kevin's permission to write about him in this book, but I'd like to chat to him. If he's offhand and doesn't want to speak, fine, but we're writing a chapter on him. So Adam spoke to him, and then Adam phoned me and said, 'Kevin wants to speak to you.' And he couldn't have been nicer to me; he was very warm on the phone – and he seemed really chuffed that we'd chosen him as one of the country's great batsmen.

"I arranged to speak to him on December 23rd at a particular time, and when I phoned on the dot he was waiting for my call. We spoke for about an hour. And we never referred back to the meeting with him and his father."

It has to be said that Pietersen, at the time of the meeting with Ali, had not shown clear signs of being a star of the future. At that point he had played only 10 first-class matches, five for KwaZulu-Natal and five for the provincial B team. He made his debut for Natal B in 1997, having been picked as an off-spinner and hard-hitting lower-order batsman. For the Natal A team in 1999–2000, he made just 104 runs, 61 of them in one innings, at an average of 26. By contrast with Graeme Smith's early record, Pietersen had not made big runs, even at provincial level. His highest score in six limited-overs matches was 11. He was regarded primarily as a bowler, but here his record was also nothing special: 14 first-class wickets at 36.85.

Did he really believe then that he could make it in the UK? "Even today I am surprised at what I achieved in the UK – in fact, incredibly surprised," he says. "All I was hoping for was that I would get an opportunity and if I performed, I knew my career would take off."

Pietersen then accepted an invitation from Clive Rice, who was coaching Nottinghamshire, to play for the county. When he got there, "Clive called me into his office and said, 'You will play every match this season. You will bat at number six and you will bowl as much as you can.' That gave me huge confidence. It was a real booster for me. It took away my insecurity."

The innings that meant the most to Pietersen in his career came in this period. It was not in Tests, but when he made 165 not out (also the first first-class century of his career) for Nottinghamshire against Middlesex at Lord's. "The night before I could not believe that I would be playing at Lord's."

He was selected for the first Ashes Test of the 2005 series, also at Lord's, and immediately made an impact for his adopted country. He made 57 in the first innings, against a very strong Australian

Kevin Pietersen: aggressive, vulnerable and flamboyant, at times he seemed to be his own worst enemy and his career was unjustly terminated

© AP Photo/Ajit Solanki/PictureNET Africa

attack. When he came to the wicket the score was 21 for five, and his contribution was the top score in a total of 155. He then led the scoring again in the second innings, making an unbeaten 64 in a total of 180. England lost the match by 239 runs; everyone but Pietersen had battled against Australia's two great bowlers, Shane Warne and Glenn McGrath. *Wisden* noted that "his treatment of McGrath was soul-stirring. It was a performance that reminded some of the arrival of another super-confident South African-born England batsman, Tony Greig, more than 30 years before." This was when Greig had taken on the West Indian and Australian fast bowlers.

Pietersen followed his two debut half-centuries with another: 71 in the second Test at Edgbaston. "England shed their inhibitions and their vulnerability," said *Wisden*, "and hurtled to 407 inside 80 overs – not the full 90 – the most conceded by Australia on the first day of any Test since 1938." England won the match by just two runs, the closest result ever in England-Australia Tests, ahead of the three-run margin at Old Trafford in 1902 and Melbourne in 1982–83.

In the final Test at the Oval, and the fifth of Pietersen's career, he made his maiden Test hundred and ensured that England would draw the match and therefore win the series – and take the Ashes for the first time in 16 years and eight series.

When Pietersen came to the wicket at the Oval on the morning of the fifth day, Ian Bell had just gone out for a duck and England were 67 for three, a lead of 73. A few quick wickets and Australia might have been able to square the series 2-2 and so retain the Ashes. But Pietersen "reeled off shots outrageous in any circumstances, unimaginable in these". By tea, he "had pulled, punched, slashed and smashed his way" to 158 in only 187 balls, at a strike rate of 84.49. While he was at the wicket 241 runs were added. "With the match – and the series – hanging in the balance," Cricinfo reported, "Pietersen strode out and belted the ball around The

Oval, not only spending precious minutes at the crease but also scoring his runs so rapidly that Australia's slim hopes of chasing a fifth-day target vanished in a trice."

From the first Test he played, there were no further questions about Pietersen's ability at the highest level; concerns over whether he was really "English" were silenced by his success. In five Tests, against a strong Australian side, he had made 473 runs at 52.55.

After 18 months and 20 Tests, he had scored 1 865 runs at an average of 50.40 at the high strike rate of 69.79, with six centuries (including, strangely, three where he made exactly 158) and seven fifties. He was regarded as both the best and most consistent batsman in the England side.

Pietersen's first double-century came in 2007 in his 25th Test, at Leeds against the West Indies. Again his strike rate was remarkable: 226 runs in 262 balls (86.25). This was the third-highest score made by an English batsman in more than a hundred years of Test cricket at Headingley. England won by an innings, with Pietersen making just 61 runs fewer than all the West Indies batsmen in the match. "For more than seven hours," wrote *Wisden*, "Pietersen punched and pummelled the West Indians like a heavyweight boxer, one very quick of foot as well as hand."

The first time Pietersen played against South Africa in a Test match was in England in 2008, when he had 39 Tests under the belt. In the drawn first game at Lord's he made an outstanding 152 in 181 balls, and with Ian Bell (199) helped England surge to 593 for eight. This was the game where South Africa followed on 346 behind, and then saved the game with centuries from Smith, McKenzie and Amla.

South Africa won the next two Tests and thereby the series, making Michael Vaughan feel compelled to resign as England captain. For the last Test of the dead rubber, won by England by six wickets, Pietersen was appointed captain of his adopted country. However, as *Wisden* put it, this was an "attempt to introduce him

into the inner sanctum, but it lasted only five months as his relationship with the coach, Peter Moores, was uncomfortable from
the outset. Their differences simmered throughout a troubled tour
of India and when the rift became public, Pietersen was forced to
resign early in the New Year of 2009, with a disenchanted Moores
sacked on the same day." Pietersen had been captain for three Tests
and 12 ODIs. Andrew Strauss took over the captaincy.

Pietersen's first (and only) Test series in South Africa was in
2009–10. The series was tied 1-1 with two matches drawn, with him
making only 177 runs in seven innings and only once passing 50.

But he remained capable of swinging a match with his fast,
aggressive scoring.

In April 2012 in the second Test in Sri Lanka, he came in after
"Cook and Strauss had blunted a modest Sri Lankan attack with
the help of Trott," reported *Wisden*. "Then Pietersen, suddenly free
as a bird, shredded the bowlers in an audacious innings of 151
from 165 balls – England's highest Test score in Sri Lanka. This
was the Pietersen of old, before the burden of captaincy and the
disappointment of losing it. He trusted his instincts, and the ball
kept disappearing over the short boundaries."

In December 2010 in the second Test in Adelaide, in the first
of three victories that regained the Ashes, Pietersen made 227 in
308 balls, as England piled up 620 runs at a run rate of 4.07 per
over. Again he shared a big partnership (175) with Cook (148), and
they set up an innings victory.

Pietersen's last Test against his former countrymen was in July
2012, when he hit 149 in the drawn second Test at Leeds. He
passed 7000 Test runs during this innings, and made his second
fifty in just 52 balls; he made 106 runs in the final session of the
third day. And he scored 64 runs off 72 balls from Dale Steyn,
the world's number one bowler. At this point he had played ten
Tests against South Africa in his career, making 817 runs at 45.38.

But this excellent innings of 149 was soon overshadowed by

controversy. In May 2012, before the series against South Africa, Pietersen had fallen out with the England authorities because he was demanding the freedom to play for longer in the Indian Premier League, and he had announced his retirement from limited-overs international cricket – and then changed his mind. The view was expressed, by officials and some players, that Kevin Pietersen seemed to think he was bigger than the team.

"As he was celebrating his 21st century," said *Wisden*, "he was pointedly waving his bat in the direction of his wife, Jessica, and only cursorily acknowledging those of his teammates who had bothered to appear on the dressing-room balcony." At the press conference after the match, Pietersen seemed to confirm a break-down in the relationship with some of his teammates. Later in the week, news broke that he had been sending text messages to his "buddies" in the South African team, making derogatory com-ments about his England teammates – in particular captain Andrew Strauss, whom he described as a *doos* (later translated by English media as a "mild Afrikaans insult"). Although he apologised, he was then dropped from the side for the third and final Test, and left out of the World T20 tournament in Sri Lanka – "England predictably struggling in his absence".

In October 2012 Strauss was asked for his views on the Pietersen affair, and on the possibility that Pietersen might return to the England side. "Well, what makes people like KP special as cricket-ers is they are different," he told the *Guardian*. "Nine-tenths of my time as England captain I found him a good guy to have in my team. He set the right example in practice and I felt he could have been far more resentful of me, in the sense that he had been removed as captain before I took over. But he just got on with his job and our relationship was pretty good – which is why it was so surpris-ing and baffling when I heard what had been going on (with the texting). In the preceding months he had not given me any hint of what he thought about me.

"It saddens me that we've been through this – after all the hard work we put in as a group for three-and-a-half years. We all genuinely believed in this special bond and chemistry we had. Unfortunately we've slipped from there and the guys are going to need to recover that. It's going to be tough.

"If they can make it work, then obviously England will be a better side with KP in it because he's an outstanding player. But if, behind the scenes, things are difficult and resentment is harboured, and if KP is not fully committed to England, there are going to be problems. But it's in everyone's interests to make it work."

Pietersen did return to the side with a short-term central contract, in November 2012, and played in six Tests against India and New Zealand. It was in this period that he produced what he regards as the best innings of his Test career (also regarded by many in the English media as the best innings for England in Asia): 186 runs in the second Test against India in Mumbai. England had lost the first Test. "It was hot and humid, the pitch was spinning," he says. "But I played the spinners very well. It was a faultless innings, no chances."

Even though the conditions were tough, Pietersen's strike rate remained impressive at 79.82, boosted by 20 fours and four sixes. He and Alistair Cook (122) shared a partnership of 206, and they both equalled the England record for most centuries scored (held by Wally Hammond, Colin Cowdrey and Geoff Boycott). Nobody else made more than 29 in an England total of 413, and spinners Monty Panesar and Graeme Swann took 19 wickets in the match. England won by 10 wickets and went on to take the series 2-1 – their first victory in India for 28 years.

Next on the schedule was the two intense back-to-back Ashes series between July 2013 and January 2014. The series in the English summer was won by England 3-0, with Pietersen batting consistently enough to justify his place, but he was below his own high standards: 388 runs at 38.80, with one century and three fifties. In Australia, however, the balance of power swung dramatically, with the hosts winning 5-0. Pietersen's batting declined and he was no longer the dominant batsman in his side: 294 runs at 29.40, with only two fifties in his ten innings. But he was still England's leading run-scorer in the series.

In early 2014, Pietersen had made 8 181 Test runs – fifth-most for England, at an average of 47.28 in 104 Tests. He was the leading run-scorer for England in all international formats combined. Whatever the prospects of his career being extended, though, it was halted by off-the-field issues. He published a sensational second book, *KP: The Autobiography*, crammed with blunt comments on various officials and players. One of his complaints was that a culture of bullying ruled the England dressing-room, led by Matt Prior, and he was viciously critical of coaches Andy Flower and Peter Moores.

"If I think something's wrong – and it's got me into trouble – my big fault is that I'm too honest, and if I think something I'll say it," he wrote. "I've fallen on the sword a few times. But also one of my good strengths is to acknowledge when I'm wrong. And I'll always say I'm sorry when I get it wrong." He said he regretted the texting affair involving Strauss, and had apologised to him.

In an interview on the book, the *Daily Telegraph* asked Pietersen if he ever felt "integrated, accepted, loved" in the England team. "Just with Duncan Fletcher (as coach), and with Michael Vaughan (as captain). That's it. I would love to know how many more runs I would have scored had Fletcher coached me throughout my career. Never if I messed up would he make me feel like it was the biggest travesty in the world. He would encourage me to continue doing stuff. My job in the England team was to win games of cricket for England. My job in the England batting order was to be aggressive, to put fear into the opposition; to take risks, calculated risks, dominate the Test match so that we could be in a position where we could win."

It was made clear after the publication of the book that Pietersen's England career was over. However, he seemed to have been thrown a lifeline when there was a change in the executive. Moores was dismissed for the second time as England coach, and incoming ECB chairman Colin Graves seemed to suggest that Pietersen might be considered again for national selection if he made runs in county cricket. Pietersen took this as a promise, gave up the chance of a lucrative contract in the Indian Premier League, and went back to play county cricket for Surrey for no pay at the start of the 2015 English season. As if he was writing the first chapter of a comeback fairy-tale, he made a big century against Oxford University; in his third match, against Leicestershire, he smashed a triple-century: 355 runs in 396 balls, taking seven and a half hours.

It was not enough. Graves denied he had promised Pietersen anything. Andrew Strauss – the former captain who had been the subject of the *doos* text in 2012, and now the director of cricket – said there were still "trust issues" with Pietersen and that he would not be selected for the upcoming series against New Zealand and Australia. Though the door was not closed on future selection, it was not clear what Pietersen might have to do to rehabilitate himself with Strauss – and at the age of 34, his prospects of a Test return seemed to be rapidly diminishing, along with his appetite for the game.

"This is outrageous," says Ali. "In the history of world cricket there have been some very difficult people. We've written about Eric Rowan in this book. Think of Syd Barnes and Geoff Boycott of England – awkward characters. The game of cricket is a mixture of different personalities – what they have in common is the game, often nothing else. Some of them are difficult, and they need leadership.

"Now in Kevin's book, very well written, he does say some very tough things about people he's played with. I think in hindsight he would say he went a bit overboard. But he's still their best batsman, a world-class player. I would have thought that with good leadership, you could get together. He could apologise, admit he went overboard, sort out all the issues, and move forward. Instead they tell him he's out of contention for another year, on the same day that he makes a 300 for Surrey.

"I must be honest. When he left initially, I was very critical of him. Other players had left South Africa to play for other countries because of apartheid – Kepler Wessels for Australia, Tony Greig and Allan Lamb for England. None of them ever criticised South Africa in the press, but Kevin did.

"Now I think, having spoken to him in December, that he's matured. And you've got to give him credit. He left this country as a spin bowler, batting number eight for Natal, and he became a world-class batsman. There's no question in my mind that Colin Graves dangled a carrot for Kevin to get back in the team – otherwise why would he have given up half a million dollars for playing in India?"

In his conversation with Ali in December 2014, Pietersen stated that "my career was a mixture of confidence – not arrogance – and anxiety and insecurity. There would be days I would feel confident at the crease and days when I would feel horrendous. In that insecure state, I would get out in no time. I was never able to conquer this problem, despite working with a psychologist."

All observers acknowledged his on-field achievements, but Pietersen the personality produced strongly divided opinions. Some thought that with sympathetic and intelligent management – as he himself felt he received with Fletcher and Vaughan – the splits in the dressing-room could have been avoided and his career prolonged.

Others argued that he had only himself to blame, and that he could hardly expect to be welcomed back after the scathing personal comments in his book. After interviewing him about one of his books, Rachel Cooke wrote in the *Guardian*: "My admiration for Pietersen as a batsman knows no bounds; he is, as Michael Vaughan has said, a kind of genius. But in person, he is very difficult … His quite outstanding charmlessness is difficult to fathom; it comes at you like a blow to the chest and leaves you shocked and winded."

Discussing his batting career, Pietersen identified the importance of a sense of control when facing the world's great bowlers. "The best fast bowler I faced was Mohammad Asif – I never felt I was in control of him. His deliveries would hit the seam regularly and you would never know which way the ball would deviate. His balls seemed to accelerate after the ball hit the pitch." Although the bowler who got his wicket most times in Tests (10) was the Australian Peter Siddle, "for the majority of them I was out to poor shots. He was a line-and-length bowler. I never felt Siddle was in control of me."

He had a different view of Muralitharan, "the best spinner I ever faced. Murali was a superstar. I would never know whether his deliveries would turn one foot, two feet, three feet. I couldn't pick out his doosra. I knew that when we played Sri Lanka, I would have to get my runs in the first innings, because I would have no chance in the second with the pitch wearing."

Technically, Pietersen was initially a strong leg-side player, with some weakness against orthodox left-arm spinners. "Being tall, I would stretch out and get my front foot to a left-arm spin bowler and, because I was so far forward, I'd be given not out when the ball hit my pad." However, with the advent of TV replays to assist the umpires, "I was being given out and was forced to hit these spinners through the off side."

The best South African batsman he played with or against was Jacques Kallis – "the best cricketer ever to have played the game". The best South African bowlers were Morné Morkel and Dale Steyn, with Morkel having the edge: "Facing him was uncomfortable because of his height and bounce. I never felt that Dale was in control of me."

Pietersen is proud of his strong work ethic. Unlike players such as Graeme Pollock and Jacques Kallis, he always practised long and very hard. "I always wanted to make practice conditions difficult – like batting on turning wickets. In the indoor nets I would get the coaches to throw bumpers at me from halfway down the pitch. I would generally bat for an hour in the nets, and I would not stop practising until I felt good. Only then would I sleep easily at night. I also used to run for hours on the road – that helped me get my mind right for the big day."

In primary and high school, Pietersen was clearly a talented player, but seen as primarily a bowler. An important early influence was Graham Ford, who later coached the Proteas: "I knew him from the age of five – he was a teacher at my primary school, and over the years he became a close family friend. He has always coached and advised me. He treats people well, he's unselfish. He would be prepared to throw you a thousand balls in the nets, if that was what you wanted. He is one of the most hard-working coaches you will ever meet."

His toughest experience in international cricket? "The Australian crowds – they are abusive and relentless. They would target me because I was England's number one batsman. In many ways it was also a sign of respect."

However, the most hostile crowd Pietersen ever encountered was when he was playing for England for the first time in South Africa, at the Wanderers in the ODI series of 2004–05. It was only his fifth ODI. "I thought if I could survive that day, I would be able to deal with any crisis in cricket down the road." If he was nervous, it did not show. *Wisden* recorded that "nobody seemed happier than Pietersen, who was there at the end after being loudly booed while walking out for his first innings against South Africa, the country he abandoned in frustration at a perceived lack of opportunities. His initial exchanges with the always theatrical André Nel provided the most dramatic moments of the game, with Pietersen struggling nervously for 11 balls before getting off the mark." He ended up making 22 not out as England won the rain-shortened match.

In six innings in that ODI series he made 454 runs (average 151), including a 75 and three centuries: 108 not out in 96 balls in Bloemfontein, in a tied game where both sides finished on 270; 100 not out off 69 balls (the fastest for England at the time) in East London, with South Africa winning by seven runs; and 116 including ten fours and six sixes at Centurion. It was as if he was making a statement about the talent that South Africa had lost. But "I always enjoyed playing against South Africa – I had some good friends in their team, and it was always a special feeling to be playing against your buddies."

"Whatever view you held," *Wisden* has written of Pietersen's international career, now apparently ended, "he deserved to be recognised as one of the most captivating cricketers to pull on an England shirt. His flamboyant stroke-play was at the heart of many of England's finest performances for a decade. A brazen belief in his own ability, moments of outrageous unorthodoxy and, at times, a surprising vulnerability on and off the field have all combined to give him great box-office appeal."

Kevin Pietersen
Born 27 June 1980
International career: 2004–2014

	M	Inns	NO	Runs	HS	Avg	SR	100	50	Conv
Tests	104	181	8	8181	227	47.28	62	23	35	39.65
First-class	217	358	26	16522	355*	49.76	69	50	71	41.32
ODIs	136	125	16	4440	130	40.73	87	9	25	26.47
List A	253	233	34	8112	147	40.76	92	15	46	24.59

PART SIX

GLITTERING IN A GOLDEN ERA

11

Hashim Amla

H ashim Amla – "Hash" to his teammates – is the first black person appointed to captain South Africa on a permanent basis. It is a rich symbolic achievement, because he is also a living bridge between apartheid South Africa and the country's democracy.

His brother, Ahmed Amla, a batsman good enough to play provincial cricket, is only four years older than Hashim but his education was different. Under the racial "own affairs" constitution that prevailed in the 1980s, he attended the all-Indian Tongaat Secondary School. "When I went to school," he told Cricinfo in 2009, "I only played with the Indian kids. You had separate exams, the whites had separate exams. The integration hadn't occurred yet. But when Hash came along, the system had changed so rapidly. That really helped him. He studied in an integrated school, played with and against white and other coloured kids. It does have a huge impact on the personality."

The national captaincy is of vital symbolic and inspirational importance in a game where whites are still seen by some observers to be calling the shots and holding back players who are not white. There is also no question of Amla's greatness as a batsman. By mid-2015 he had played 82 Tests, scoring 6757 runs. His average of 52.78 was better than that of any other South African batsman except Jacques Kallis, Graeme Pollock and Dudley Nourse.

Amla is the only South African to have scored a triple-century in Tests, as well as two double-centuries. He is a great accumulator of runs – but he can also score them under pressure of time. At the end of the 2015 World Cup, Amla had scored 20 ODI centuries in 112 innings – one every 5.6 innings on average. This is better than any other player who has scored 15 or more centuries, placing him well ahead on the all-time list of, for example, AB de Villiers (8.95), Sachin Tendulkar (9.22), Chris Gayle (12.05) and Ricky Ponting (12.17).

Born in Durban, Amla grew up in Tongaat, a town where the dominant community was of Indian descent. His father had a medical practice there. He attended two local primary schools and then, after a year at Tongaat Secondary, he moved to Durban High School (DHS) for the last four years of high school. For three of those years he had to travel in to Durban every day from Tongaat – a round trip of 80 kilometres. In his matric year he stayed in Durban.

Amla's prodigious talent and calm temperament were obvious at an early age, as he followed in the footsteps of great DHS old boys like Trevor Goddard, Barry Richards and Lee Irvine. He scored freely at junior level and played in representative teams with future Proteas teammates AB de Villiers and JP Duminy. Amla also emerged early as a leader: he captained the DHS 1st XI and played for SA Schools in his matric year; in 2002 he captained the South African Under-19 side in the final of the World Cup for that age group.

There was always something rather different about Amla's technique. He seemed to draw on his subcontinental genes, rather than the cricket culture of South Africa. "He reminds me very strongly of Mohammad Azharuddin," says Ali, referring to the dazzling Indian captain who was at his peak in the 1990s. "Hashim has very strong wrists. He has this ability to whip balls on the wicket to the leg side. I haven't seen any other South African players like that. It's as if he had been plucked out of Hyderabad."

Amla's technique was a source of controversy when he was picked for the national side. He seemed a natural choice for the Proteas after his performance in domestic cricket in 2004–05: he was the only man to exceed 1 000 runs in the first-class season, at an average of 50.15 and including five centuries.

"I played one Test in India in November 2004. I made 24 and 2, and then I was dropped," Amla recalls. "The story was that my technique was not good enough, because my back-lift was coming from gully." He missed the first Test in the five-match home series against England, and was then brought back for two Tests over the 2004–05 Christmas and New Year holiday. Again he failed, making 1, 0, 25 and 10. At this point his average was 10.33 from six innings, and again he was dropped.

In conversation with Ali, Amla discussed the "twirl" that he executes as he brings down the bat to play a delivery. "I don't know how that developed, to be honest. My coaching was very orthodox from a young age. But it may have come from when we were growing up – my brother and I used to play cricket in a little courtyard. I now realise that I used to take up my stance very close to the wall, and maybe there was no space behind me for a conventional back-lift."

Amla took the criticisms seriously and set to work to straighten his back-lift. "I was adamant at that time that I had to try and sort out the back-lift – just get it done. The whole off-season we were in the nets trying to get it right. I was being slated because my technique wasn't good enough. They were saying that I should never have been picked in the first place for South Africa, that I was only a quota player."

However, Amla continued to score heavily in domestic cricket. In March 2005, two months after he had been dropped from the national side, he made his maiden double-century in the Supersport Series final, finishing on 249 in 11 hours. In the 2005–06 domestic season, he was again the leading run-scorer in the Supersport Series. He thought his off-season work on changing his technique had paid off.

But after one of Amla's big innings, Phil Russell, the KwaZulu-Natal Dolphins coach, pointed out to him that he was still using the twirl in his back-lift. "Phil said to me, 'You're scoring so many runs with your technique, why do you want to change it? Why try to fix something that's not broken? If you're making runs, nobody talks about your technique.' This was the best piece of advice I ever got."

Not everyone had been calling for Amla to fix his back-lift. "Don't worry about his technique," Gary Kirsten said at the time to writer Richard Calland. "Bradman picked his bat up towards gully. At this level, it's all about temperament, and anyone who can score 250 in a Supersport Series final has got what it takes."

Kirsten's reference to the greatest batsman of all, Donald Bradman, is validated by what Bradman wrote in his book *The Art of Cricket*, published in 1958: "Reams of matter have been written about the necessity of taking one's bat back perfectly straight. Some coaching books even advocate taking the bat back towards the stumps. Don't let me be misunderstood. I am all in favour of a straight bat at the right time and place, but technique must be the servant, not the master. Too many players fail because their thoughts are concentrated on where their left elbow is, or where something else is, instead of hitting the ball. I was never conscious of my back-lift and I did not take any particular notice where the bat went until I saw movie shots of me in action. It was clear that my initial bat movement was towards second slip."

Having missed 12 Tests against Zimbabwe, the West Indies and Australia, and 14 months after his failures against India and England, Amla was brought back to the national side for two Tests against New Zealand. He replaced Herschelle Gibbs, who was described as "mentally tired".

The first Test was at Newlands and it started on 27 April 2006 – later in the year than any other Test had been played at the ground. The reason was that the New Zealand matches had to be moved

Hashim Amla: strong, elegant and wristy, his unruffled manner concealed an ability to score both heavily and quickly, as demonstrated by his remarkable statistics

forward to accommodate an international tournament later in the year.

The Western Cape in winter is not an ideal place for cricket. Play was delayed on the first day by a wet outfield, and ended early because of bad light. On the second day, blow-torches had to be used to dry the bowlers' footholes, and Table Mountain was made invisible by fog. In these conditions a draw was almost inevitable.

New Zealand made 593 for eight declared; South Africa replied with 513. Amla top-scored with 149 runs off 317 balls. "It was quite a relief," he told Cricinfo. "I felt that I was under quite a lot of pressure and I was fortunate to have Boeta Dippenaar there, and then Jacques Kallis. He's a fantastic influence at the crease, very calm and collected, and he helped me through some tough patches."

Again the question came up about his technique. "I spoke to several top coaches, and they all told me to keep it as natural as possible. When I'm batting, I try to concentrate on what I'm doing and stay as calm as I can. I always try to keep it simple. I was disappointed to go out on 149 – no one wants to go out on 149. But I was happy with my first century. I hope it will be a long Test career, and maybe if I can score 50 centuries in my career, nobody will question my technique."

After his big maiden century, Amla got a half-century in the next Test in Johannesburg (another first: a Test match in May, at a Wanderers stadium that was frost-bitten in the mornings). Amla's 56 was the second-highest score in a total of 181, after Smith's 63; only three other players made double figures. But New Zealand had batted first and scored only 119, and South Africa went on to win the match by four wickets.

It seemed Amla had now proved himself at the highest level. But then followed a sequence of scores where he made 431 runs in 21 Test innings, with only four 50s, at an average of just 21.55. In November 2007, going into another two-match home series against New Zealand, he was expecting to be dropped if he did not perform.

South Africa went in first at the Wanderers, "after boldly choosing to bat on a threatening pitch featuring both grass and cracks", and Amla made only 12 in a total of 226. New Zealand replied with 118, and before South Africa's second innings, Amla sensed he was running out of time. "There was a feeling within the team, I think, and in the media that this was going to be my last knock," he told Ali. But at the end of the second day he was at the crease with 85 not out, having come in with the score on eight for one, and South Africa was 179 for two. This gave them a lead of 287, an ideal situation for taking the pressure off the batsmen. "That night I had a beautiful sleep. I was pretty much content to accept whatever happened the next day. It was the best sleep of my life, I had no anxiety."

The next day Amla reached an unbeaten 176 – the innings that he still regards as having meant the most to him in his career. He took eight and a half hours in all, sharing a massive partnership of 330 for the third wicket with Jacques Kallis. They enabled a declaration at 422 for three. Dale Steyn took 10 for 93 in the match, and South Africa won by 358 runs.

"Amla's credentials as a number three, severely questioned before this series," said *Wisden*, "were enhanced with every minute he spent at the crease." When asked afterwards what effect the innings might have on his career, he replied with typical under-statement: "It should keep me in the team for the next game." Luck had also been on his side – he was dropped when he had just two.

In the second Test at Centurion, Amla (103) and Kallis (131) each made a second successive century and carried on where they'd left off at the Wanderers, with a third-wicket partnership of 220. They became the eighth pair to produce consecutive Test partnerships of over 200. "Occasionally Amla would flick a half-volley through midwicket with the speed of a chameleon catching flies with its tongue," said *Wisden*. His solidity enabled Kallis, freed at last of the responsibility of anchoring the innings, to cut loose, so that the run rate in a total of 383 was nearly four per over. With Steyn again rampant, South Africa won by an innings inside three days.

At this point of his career, Amla had played 17 Tests and his two centuries against New Zealand had pulled his average into the thirties (33.50).

Six Tests later, against India at Chennai in March 2008, Amla made 240 runs in the match – 159 and 81. His fourth Test century helped South Africa to a total of 540. "It was a good wicket to bat on," Amla said, "but they were the hottest conditions I've ever batted in. That was the most difficult challenge. It is always special to score a hundred in the subcontinent, it gives you a lot of confidence. It is a special moment because it came away from home." This was a high-scoring draw: Amla's achievement was overshadowed by Virender Sehwag's spectacular triple-century: 319 runs in 304 balls.

Four months later, in the 2008 four-Test series in England, Amla made 104 not out in the first game at Lord's, as South Africa fought back astonishingly to salvage a draw by making 393 for three declared after following on. Apart from 76 in the last Test, however, he otherwise had a quiet series. Much the same applied to the back-to-back series against Australia – three Tests there and three in South Africa – between December 2008 and March 2009: he made 406 runs at 40.60 in 11 innings, moderate by his own high standards.

Amla's next major milestone was his first double-century: an unbeaten 253 not out against India in Nagpur, in February 2010. He took more than 11 hours – 675 minutes – which was the second-longest innings for South Africa after Gary Kirsten's 878-minute 275 against England in Durban. "With Amla using his marvellous wrists to manipulate the ball all around the ground," said *Wisden*, "he was remorseless, showing tremendous shot selection and powers of concentration."

The *Hindu* newspaper wrote that "there was a time (in the past) when Amla's movements at the crease resembled those of a marionette dangled on strings: the bat descended after a loopy double-take; the feet limply straddled the crease. Amla has since tidied his game, refining his back-lift, strengthening his footwork. It's still a refreshingly unique method, but as he showed in Nagpur, it's grown more robust. Amla's pull stroke, for instance, was fraught with risk earlier; the simplification of the back-lift has helped him execute the stroke with greater control."

South Africa made 558 for six declared in their first innings; Amla was on the field for all but five of those runs. Steyn took 10 for 108 in the match and South Africa won by an innings and six runs.

It is hard to top a double-century, but immediately there was more to come from Amla. In the second Test at Kolkata, he made a century in each innings (114 and 123 not out), in the process scoring more than 40 per cent of his team's runs in the entire match. It was not enough to save his side, though: India made 643 for six in their first innings and won by an innings and 57 runs, thus levelling the two-match series.

So Amla had passed three figures in three successive innings, for a total of 490 runs for only once dismissed. That gave him a series average of 490 – only England's Wally Hammond had done better, with 563 runs for once out in two Tests in New Zealand in 1932–33.

Amla then went into a brief slump against the West Indies, making only 122 runs in three Tests. In November 2010, he returned to form in the drawn first match of a two-Test series against Pakistan in Dubai, making 80 and 118 not out. In South Africa's second innings of 318 for two, Amla shared yet another double-century partnership (242) with Kallis. In the second Test in Dubai he made 62.

Next on the Test schedule was a home series against India in the 2010–11 season, where he averaged exactly 50 in three Tests, scoring 250 runs with one century. That was followed by a break from Test cricket for South Africa of nearly a year.

Unusually for a leading batsman, Amla made his ODI debut more than three years after he first played Tests. He had been regarded as a reliable accumulator rather than a fast scorer. He did not play in the 2007 World Cup. In the 2011 tournament, he made 306 runs at an average of 43.71 – but more than a third of his runs came from the 113 he made against minnows Bangladesh.

Going into the two-Test series against Australia in South Africa in November 2011, much was expected of Amla, now a veteran of 51 Tests. He had hauled his Test average up to 46.95 from nearly 4 000 runs, having scored a century on average once every 7.5 innings. He did not disappoint, scoring two centuries in his four innings.

The first Test at Newlands was filled with astonishing scenes. Australia batted first and made a solid 284 (Michael Clarke 151), being all out after 90 minutes on the second morning. In the half-hour before lunch South Africa reached 49 for one. Telford Vice related in *Wisden* that "Gary Kirsten, South Africa's coach, took that as his cue to go home and spend a few hours with his wife, Deborah, and their new-born daughter. When Kirsten returned to the ground for the last hour of the day, he struggled to believe a scoreboard that alleged South Africa were 72 for one. 'Has it been raining?' he asked when he reached the dressing-room. 'Um, no, coach,' was the gentle reply. 'We're in the second innings.'"

After lunch South Africa had crashed from 49 for one wicket to 96 all out. Amla made three, and only two batsmen, the openers, reached double figures. South Africa trailed by 188 runs and looked headed for certain defeat.

Yet after another 18 overs, Australia had been shot out by Steyn, Philander (five for 15) and Morkel for just 47 runs, their lowest score in Tests since 1902. At one stage they were 21 for nine wickets – the lowest Test score by any team with just one wicket standing. It was only the second Test match in history where at least part of all four innings took place on the same day: on November 10th, Australia started the day on 214 for eight; South Africa were all out for 96, followed by Australia being all out for 47; and then South Africa reached 81 for one at the close.

Absurdly, after being completely written off, South Africa needed 236 to win. Even though there were still three days to go – a required run rate of less than one per over – Graeme Smith (101 not out) and Amla (112) batted aggressively and scored at a rate of more than four an over to seal an eight-wicket victory with well over two days to spare.

In the second Test, in Johannesburg, South Africa lost a thriller – in which the run rate for all four innings was well over three runs per over – by two wickets.

Australia led by 30 runs on the first innings. When South Africa batted again, Amla top-scored with 105 out of a total of 339. Australia needed 310 to win – the highest fourth-innings target ever at the Wanderers. It seemed that they would not make it when they lost their sixth wicket at 215, still 95 runs short with only four wickets remaining. But then Brad Haddin and Mitchell Johnson frustrated the bowlers with a stand of 72, and the score moved tantalisingly to 287 for seven, then 292 for eight. Australia hung on to scrape together the remaining 18 runs.

Amla's next major innings – the one that will probably remain the innings of his life – was his triple-century in the English summer of 2012.

In the first Test at the Oval, England batted first for a respectable 385 all out, and South Africa ended the second day on 89 for one, with Amla and Graeme Smith at the crease. On the third day South Africa added a massive 317 runs for the loss of one wicket: Smith for 131, after he and Amla had made 259 for the second wicket.

Having batted the whole day, after spending 37 overs at the crease the previous day, Amla was on 183 at the close.

The next day he moved steadily to the triple-century. "I'm happy, surprised, really excited that I managed to do something that has never been done before as a South African," he said. "With my scoring rate, 300 is usually a very long way away, so it didn't cross my mind until I'd got to 250. I'm overwhelmed. It's a lovely feeling." In fact, Amla was being hard on himself regarding his scoring rate. By the end of that Oval match, his Test career strike rate was 51.63 runs per 100 balls – comparable at that stage to renowned batsmen like AB de Villiers (54.92), Graeme Smith (59.84) and Jacques Kallis (45.79). Perhaps Amla's calm demeanour at the crease gives the impression that he is scoring slowly – the facts often say otherwise.

Amla and Kallis took South Africa to a record Test total, for two or fewer wickets, of 637 for two declared. Their partnership for the third wicket was 377 – the tenth time they'd put on a hundred together, including six partnerships over 200 and three over 300. South Africa won the match by an innings and 12 runs – only the fifth time in Test history that a team had won a match losing only two wickets.

Amla's innings was "unforgettable for its calmness, placement and concentration," said *Wisden*. "On the attack, he was strong, elegant and wristy; while his defence, forward or back, was neat, fluent and commanding. No single shot stood out, but that was testament to his all-round dominance … it came away from home, against the team rated best in the world." He was on the field for the entire match, except for the 11 minutes it took Alviro Petersen to make 0 before Amla came in.

This was the first triple-century in England since Graham Gooch made 333 at Lord's in 1990, and the first by a foreign batsman since Bobby Simpson's 311 for Australia at Old Trafford in 1964. Only Don Bradman and Brian Lara have scored more runs against England in a single innings.

Of Amla's 311, Gooch said: "It was a wonderful effort. You need a great attitude, good technique, good knowledge and above all spot-on concentration. He showed all four things today." Commentator Mark Nicholas wrote that "the secret to Amla's play is his use of wrists, which allow late contact with the ball and no loss of power. The Oval pitch was slow but the Indian in him transcended it.

"His footwork is a paragon of economy," continued Nicholas. "Nothing is exaggerated, bar the quirky back-lift that many a coach has studied before concluding against the suggestion of change ... He plays with softly held hands but firm wrists that confirm the blade straight at impact, allowing the transferred weight of the body to create the power ... The whiplash effect is remarkable, not unlike that created by Mohammad Azharuddin, and is finished by a dramatic follow-through that wraps the bat around the surprisingly narrow shoulders of the executioner."

A legend arose after Amla's marathon innings that he had achieved it without eating or drinking during the day, because the Oval match took place in the Muslim fast month of Ramadan. This wasn't true: he used one of the dispensations available. "Because I'm travelling away from home I don't have to fast," he said. "But I will make it up when I get home."

Amla's 311 was at the centre of the team's big victory at the Oval. He again played a vital role in the third Test at Lord's, which England needed to win in order to level the series. The teams were separated by only six runs on the first innings. In South Africa's second innings, all the batsmen struggled except Amla, who made 121 in a total of 351, while nobody else got fifty. It was an innings that made all the difference: South Africa won the Test by 51 runs and the series 2-0, and so took the number one Test ranking from England.

Three months later the Proteas went to Australia, for three Tests in the month of November. Amla made 104 in the rain-induced draw in Brisbane, sharing another century stand with Kallis in the process. The second Test was also drawn, so the series depended on the third game in Perth.

South Africa led by 62 runs on the first innings, after both sides had achieved a run rate of just over three per over. Then the Proteas cut loose in the second innings. Scoring at more than five runs an over, they made 569 all out. Amla made 196, "superbly organised and paced as always, but audacious too, manufacturing strokes, manipulating fields and generally running the show". Amla describes this as the most enjoyable knock of his career. He shared in partnerships of 178 with Smith and 149 with AB de Villiers. They set Australia an impossible target of 632, and the match was won by 309 runs – South Africa's biggest ever victory against Australia.

Amla maintained his good form with two centuries and four fifties in 12 Test innings against New Zealand, Pakistan and India. Then came another eagerly awaited contest against Australia, who were still smarting from their home defeat a year before.

In the three-Test series in February–March 2014, Australia won at Centurion as Amla made 17 and 35. The balance shifted back to South Africa at St George's Park, where Amla made a duck in a first-innings total of 423, enough for a lead of 177. In the second innings, Amla made an unbeaten 127 in 270 for five declared, setting up an easy victory for South Africa. Australia easily won the third Test at Newlands (Amla 38 and 41), and the series 2-1.

Graeme Smith had scores of 10, 4, 9, 14, 5 and 3 in this series for a dismal series average of 7.5. Dogged by chronic injury and apparently also affected by personal issues, he announced his retirement and Amla was appointed to captain the Test team. This was a natural step, given his batting achievements, his seniority in the side and his previous captaincy experience at junior representative level. He had earlier not wanted to be considered for the national role, but now he felt the time was right.

Amla took to the job calmly and with confidence, and impressed with the quality of thoughtful analysis and his composure in after-match interviews and other media interactions. He captained the Proteas in six Tests between July 2014 and January 2015, against Sri Lanka (two), Zimbabwe (one) and the West Indies, for a record of four wins and two draws. It was clear that leadership had not affected his batting: he made 543 runs in nine innings, twice not out, at an average of 77.57.

He passed 100 twice. There was an unbeaten 139 in eight hours against Sri Lanka in Colombo, which helped his team to a nail-biting draw when they ended on 159 for eight in 111 overs – their slowest batting in 15 years. But the draw also secured their first Test series win in Sri Lanka since 1993 – a major achievement for Amla in his second Test as captain.

His other big innings was his 208 against the West Indies in the first Test at Centurion, in South Africa's total of 552 for five declared. It was Amla's third innings beyond 200. He took nearly eight hours and shared a partnership of 308 with AB de Villiers. That helped South Africa to their second-biggest victory ever, by an innings and 220 runs after Dale Steyn destroyed the West Indian batting with six for 34 in their second innings.

The series against the West Indies was Amla's first at home as captain. "Having made my captaincy debut overseas, I didn't have the hype and the attention, which probably was a good thing because now I am a bit more settled," he said. "Captaining at home will be something special." A convincing 2-0 series win was the outcome.

He has shown every sign of being at home in the role. "I do enjoy captaincy. It's true that previously I preferred to concentrate on batting, not having to worry about anything else," he told Ali. "What I've learnt is that I've got to manage time wisely. That is one of the reasons I am batting at number four. It gives me little bit of extra time gathering my thoughts before going in to bat. That's been my biggest challenge so far but it's getting better and I'm sure with every series, I will learn.

"But I had captained through my whole career – and I had a great example to follow. We had Graeme as captain for ten years – in fact, the whole time I was in the team – and in many ways it was a great learning for all of us. He was a great leader. He led from the front, he was phenomenal. He didn't have to command the respect of the players, he just had the respect – through perform-ance, and just the way he managed the team."

In his conversation with Amla, Ali remarked: "I don't think I've seen any fast bowler look at you, or the bowlers and the fielders sledge you … is that right?" Amla laughed. "They used to make comments a bit – in New Zealand, England. Not so much now – a few years ago the authorities tried to clean up the sledging. It's never worried me, and when they see that, the opposition eventually give up." In his powers of concentration and ability to ignore distraction, Amla is very like Jacques Kallis; it is no wonder that they reinforced each other, and have produced so many big partnerships.

The best fast bowler Amla believes he has faced is Mohammad Asif. "His accuracy was immaculate, swing and seam. On any wicket he was difficult. Every ball he was asking a question to get you out." The best spinner he encountered was the Sri Lankan Muttiah Muralitharan. "I faced him very early in my career. He got me out a couple of times." This was in Amla's sixth and seventh Tests, both in Colombo – he was stumped for 19 and lbw for 40. "I probably would play him differently now, but then I had no idea what he was bowling. As it happened, I never played against him again."

A triple-century, a Test average of 52.78, an ODI average of 55.26, the national captaincy – what else is left for Amla to achieve? The one honour that is missing is a World Cup tournament victory.

By the time of the most recent World Cup tournament in Australasia in 2015, Amla had played 107 ODIs and had put paid to any lingering ideas that he was a slow scorer, or somehow not suited to the shorter format. He had made 5 359 runs at an average of 56.41, at the excellent strike rate of 89.41, and with 19 centuries and 27 fifties. In four ODIs against that weak West Indies side, just before the World Cup, he made 66, 153 not out, 61 not out and 133 – at an average of 206.5.

However, he could not turn that form into runs in the 2015 World Cup. With only one century (159 against Ireland) and one fifty, he made 333 runs at an average of 41.52. In the knockout stages, where South Africa beat Sri Lanka and lost to New Zealand, he made just 16 and 10.

It is not surprising, therefore, given his excellent record in ODIs overall but a moderate one in two World Cup tournaments, that Amla's remaining major ambition is "to be part of a World Cup-winning team". It was a goal that eluded the great Jacques Kallis. Amla is now 32, and has every intention of being around when the next tournament takes place in 2019. Meanwhile, he will continue to fill the hearts of bowlers with despair as he comes to the wicket in any format of the game.

Hashim Amla
Born 31 March 1983
International career: 2004–2015

	M	Inns	NO	Runs	HS	Avg	SR	100	50	Conv
Tests	82	141	13	6757	311*	52.78	52	23	28	45.09
First-class	186	306	28	14318	311*	51.50	52	44	69	38.93
ODIs	118	115	9	5743	159	54.17	89	20	28	41.66
List A	174	169	11	7424	159	46.98	87	23	39	37.09

As at 20 July 2015

12

AB de Villiers

The Wanderers had never seen anything like it – nor had any other stadium in the world. On 18 January 2015, in a match against the West Indies, AB de Villiers shattered the record for the fastest ODI century – 31 balls, five fewer than the previous record. He also hit the fastest fifty (16 balls). He smashed 16 sixes and nine fours in his 149, which meant that 88 per cent of his runs came in boundaries. In 59 minutes at the crease, he faced just 44 balls, three of which were dot balls and two were leg-byes – so that made it 39 scoring shots, an average of nearly four runs *per ball*.

South Africa also broke their own record at the Wanderers – 438 for nine against Australia in 2005, in the match billed as "the greatest ODI ever played" – by piling up 439, four short of the world record total of 443. It was also the first time three centuries had been scored in an ODI innings (the others were by Rilee Rossouw and Hashim Amla).

"None of the West Indian bowlers were spared as De Villiers put on his full range of strokes," wrote Firdose Moondia for Cricinfo. "There was the pull, the scoop, the lofted drive and the good old slog and Jason Holder, given the toughest of examinations as a young captain, was hardest hit. De Villiers plundered 45 runs off the nine balls he faced from him, including six of his sixes."

"It was mesmerising stuff," wrote Stuart Hess in *The Star*. "Never mind the straight drives delivered at 140km/hour plus, what about the legside flick, while down on one knee, against fast bowler Andre

Russell? De Villiers performed that trick twice, slapping him over backward square leg for six."

Observers searched for comparisons among the great batsmen of the past and struggled to find them. Perhaps *The Times*'s John Woodcock's comment on the swashbuckling England batsman Denis Compton, made long before De Villiers's innings, comes closest: "His feet never needed to be informed what to do and, if they got him into a tangle, his instincts usually got him out of it. He could feather a late cut from three yards down the pitch, or drive past cover point's left hand from a foot outside the leg stump or sweep when he seemed to be standing on gully's toes. If he were to come out and play against Shane Warne, the cricket would bring the country to a standstill."

De Villiers did play against Warne, but describes it as "a bit of an unfair contest. I would have loved to play against Warne when I was 28 or 30. He was amazing – a very intimidating bowler to face. On my first tour to Australia, I was 21 – he got me out bowled for 68. He was the best I have faced, with what he brought to the table: that experience, his control, the body language, the verbal intimidation. But I was young and I had no chance!" In Test cricket, De Villiers scored 34 runs off Warne and was out four times for an average of 8.50.

South Africa outclassed the West Indies in all the Tests and ODIs in early 2015 – the Proteas' last opportunity to sharpen their form before the World Cup in Australasia. Hopes were high for the tournament. De Villiers, now the ODI captain after the retirement of Graeme Smith, started with scores of 25 and 30. Then he repeated his demolition of the West Indies with an unbeaten 162 in just 66 balls. The uncomfortable thought arose that the islanders had not been competitive on tour in South Africa, thus inflating the South Africans' idea of their own ability and form going into the World Cup.

De Villiers followed that big century with scores of 24, 77 and 99, but he was not required to bat in the excellent win against

Sri Lanka in the quarter-finals. South Africa, with Kyle Abbott outstanding with the new ball, applied pressure from the start of the Sri Lankan innings and never allowed it to ease. Abbott conceded only 27 runs in his 10 overs, which prepared the way for spinners JP Duminy (three for 29) and Imran Tahir (four for 26). Sri Lanka could make only 133 and South Africa won by nine wickets.

For the semi-final against New Zealand, the form team of the tournament, Abbott was left out for Vernon Philander, who was rusty after an absence through injury. This made no sense to anyone except in terms of transformation – it was widely believed, and never specifically confirmed or denied, that Philander had been included to bring the number of black players to four. De Villiers never commented on the issue, but was said to be furious that his best bowler from the quarter-final had been left out. It did not help that Dale Steyn had not been at his best in the World Cup.

Even so, the semi-final went down to the second-last ball. In an innings shortened by rain, South Africa made 281 for five in 43 overs. It was felt they had got the worst of the Duckworth-Lewis calculation, especially as De Villiers was perfectly placed on 65 from 45 balls to score heavily in the last seven overs. New Zealand lost six wickets in reaching their target of 299 – with Steyn conceding 76 runs for just one wicket in his 8.5 overs, and Philander none for 52 in his eight overs. De Villiers could hardly have done more as a batsman, but once again World Cup glory eluded South Africa.

By the time of his great centuries against the West Indies in early 2015, De Villiers was a mature veteran of 10 years of international cricket, and acknowledged as the best all-format batsman in the world. Such is his all-round sporting ability that he could have achieved a similar status in rugby, golf or tennis.

"I played a lot of tennis," De Villiers said in conversation with Ali. "It was probably my strongest sport growing up. We went all over the country, my mom and I, playing in the various tournaments. I was number one or two in the country at under 12 and under 14 level – and then, when I was 14, I stopped tennis and I never touched a racquet again. That's when cricket took over. I don't know if it was a good or a bad thing. But I believe our schools in SA are just not well enough equipped, and the coaching is not good enough, for the guys to come through as leading tennis players. I felt I was wasting my time playing tennis. I wanted to play rugby and cricket.

"Golf – I was a scratch golfer when I was about 13. I stopped playing seriously when I was about 15. I stopped practising. I was a boarder at Affies and there was just no time – and of course there were no golf facilities at the school. So golf and tennis became a no-go at school – but I love both sports. I will never miss a major tournament in either of them. I will watch the Masters up until five in the morning if necessary."

There was also the story that he broke six national school swimming records, but "that's all nonsense," he told Ali. "Someone started that on social media and it's now regarded as fact."

De Villiers's father was a medical doctor in the rural town of Warmbaths (now Bela Bela), and so De Villiers was enrolled as a boarder at Afrikaanse Seuns Hoërskool (Affies) in Pretoria, one of the country's leading boys' schools.

"That was probably the five most important and enjoyable years of my life so far," says De Villiers. "Sport, discipline, learning how to cope on your own, taking responsibility and taking ownership for your decisions – I learned so much, and enjoyed it so much. Dr Pierre Edwards was the headmaster. He was an amazing leader. Discipline was the most important thing at his school. I loved that. I enjoy a good structure, and that is what I got there. Also important was the team spirit, and the tradition and the culture, that has all built up since the school was established in 1920.

"I grew up with a vision of lifting some major trophy – not for myself but for the team. I loved my tennis, but I always had this special feeling for a team sport. I was a boarder – Mom and Dad

AB de Villiers: master of every stroke in the book – and several that are not in the book – he may turn out to be the greatest in all forms of the game

were not there very often. Although I did go home most weekends, I generally had to make my own decisions. So after I left school, it was a little bit easier to do my own thing.

"I discovered freedom within the structure, too. That's another thing I learned from Gary Kirsten. The way he coached India was to really free the guys up. And then he came to us and did the same thing – not coaching us, but just giving the guys wings to make mistakes and to learn from their own mistakes. There are so many coaches that try to teach you how to do things – and Gary gets that really right. It goes hand in hand with what I learned at Affies."

De Villiers played rugby for the Affies 1st XV and at Craven Week for the Bulls – but he was a very late developer in this sport. "I really loved my rugby. In primary school I had always played in the best team; I was the captain and one of the best players. At high school, though, I was too small. I slotted into the under 14F team. And the coach said that physically I just wasn't there.

"I always felt my skills were good enough and I could get away with being a little smaller than the rest of the boys. But I played in the lower teams and I wasn't used to that kind of thing – I was a first-team boy! So in grade 10 I decided I was done with rugby and I was going to play hockey. I played under 16A hockey – and in that year it was the first time ever we beat Pretoria Boys' High under 16A. Before that our A team had played their C or D team. But this time the coaches pushed us up and said we could play Boys' High strength v strength – and we beat them.

"But I missed rugby so much. In grade 11 I went back – same story again, big disappointment, fifth and sixth teams at first – but then I was moved up to the 4th XV. Then the flyhalf for the third team got injured for one match towards the end of the season, and I got a chance. For some reason the 1st XV coach was there that day and he watched me play for the thirds. And he said straight-away he wanted me in the 2nd XV – and I had one game against

Boys' High. There was a massive crowd at their ground. And I had the game of my life – I slotted all seven of my kicks, made a couple of tries, and the next minute I was in the 1st XV. So it all happened in about three weeks."

The focus for De Villiers was ultimately on cricket, however. He made his debut for the Northern Titans in 2003, and for South Africa against England in December 2004. At times he justified his early promise. In his fifth Test in that series against England at Centurion, he made 92 and 109 in the opener's position. In his tenth Test, in Bridgetown in April 2005, he made 178 to help his team to an innings victory. But all too often, his promising starts fizzled out. In his first 30 ODI games, he passed 40 just nine times for an average of 31.37.

The innings that meant the most to him, De Villiers told Ali, was the 174 he made at Leeds in the second Test of the 2008 series in England. "That was a big year for me. That was when I really started feeling that I knew my game. The first four years of my international career felt like a bit of a flash in the pan. I was trying to go on instinct, not really understanding my weaknesses yet or my strengths. Those first few years were very frustrating and difficult. Going into that series in England, my batting average was about 35 in Tests and about 29 in ODIs. I thought I wasn't getting anywhere. I always felt I had the talent, I just didn't know my game well enough.

"But that's where everything changed, right there in that innings at Headingley. In the first Test at Lord's I had got a 42 in the first innings and then I just gave my wicket away. I went into the second Test very motivated.

"We bowled first. There was a big incident. I was standing at third slip. Andrew Strauss nicked a ball that came in low in front of me – it was one of those reflex catches, somehow I picked it up with my right hand and it ended up in my left hand. I was pretty sure I'd taken the catch, although I went straight to Graeme Smith and said I'm not a hundred per cent sure. He said. 'Don't worry, it's being referred.'"

The incident was replayed on the big screen – it showed clearly that the ball had bounced short.

"The whole crowd went crazy, started booing me, and through the whole Test match they were on my case. But there was no way I was going to let Straussy walk off without telling the umpires I wasn't sure. I was very happy it was referred and given not out, because I would never have been able to go to bed at night if I'd known he had to walk off the field to a non-catch."

England made 203 and the match seemed evenly poised when De Villiers, batting at number six, came in with the score on 143 for four. "When I walked in to bat, they were all booing and chanting, 'Cheater!' I was still a young guy, 24 years old, and I felt immense pressure. It was the first time I'd ever been booed walking out and that was very disappointing. I didn't feel I deserved that. It hurt quite a lot.

"But I was also very motivated by the pressure. I had more energy than ever in that innings. England were the number one team in the world at that stage. Steve Harmison was the number one bowler. It was quite difficult – and I got through it. I faced a helluva lot of balls, more than ever, but I just stuck it out. In the past I would probably have given it away."

There were tough periods in the innings, which lasted over eight hours. De Villiers was becalmed on 99 for 40 minutes, including a "not out" decision on a huge appeal by Andrew Flintoff for caught behind. "I did get my fair share of words at that, but that's part of the game. If anything, it played into my hands and motivated me to stay there for as long as possible."

Commentators noted a change in De Villiers's approach. "He has changed as a batsman from the dashing, ultra-aggressive figure who made his debut against England in 2004–05," said Cricinfo. "That series was a microcosm of his early career, as he was shunted up and down the order (and even kept wicket). He has adapted his play and this was the slowest of his six Test centuries, taking 264 balls, showing a new level of maturity."

De Villiers took more than eight hours (512 minutes) over his 174, and put on 212 for the fifth wicket with Ashwell Prince (149). "It's important on any English wicket to leave well. You have to know where your off stump is and where you want to score. I was lucky at stages and played and missed a bit, but that's part of the game." South Africa made 522 and went on to win by 10 wickets.

"That's when I realised I could score big hundreds. I was so motivated. After I got to the century, I decided, 'I'm not finished yet.' I never used to be that player – one who gets big hundreds. I was always good for a flashy 60 or 80, maybe a hundred here or there, and that's it."

In fact De Villiers had already scored a Test double-century: an unbeaten 217 out of 494 for seven declared, against India earlier that year in Ahmedabad. "De Villiers was the most fluent batsman, tackling pace and spin with aplomb," said *Wisden*, and South Africa won by an innings and 90 runs. But it was the Headingley innings four months later that he credited as marking his shift of attitude.

Ahmedabad was also the venue for the innings he regards as his best, in February 2010: an ODI century scored off just 58 balls, the sixth-fastest in history at the time. "It was a flawless knock. I just didn't make any mistakes. Very rarely has it happened to me that I've got going from the first ball of an innings, but it did that day."

De Villiers also remembers that match for being offered the opportunity to begin taking a leadership role. "Graeme Smith had gone home from the tour with a broken finger or something. Before he left he said he had plans for me to be one of the big leaders on the team one day. I'd never thought about that. Jacques Kallis was actually captain on the day, but before the game I was asked to do a little speech to the team, which I'd never had to do before. I felt I had to back up my chat with a performance – and it worked out nicely that day with my unbeaten 102. And I thought that I'd actually like to be captain someday."

De Villiers's highest Test score was the 278 not out he made against Pakistan at Abu Dhabi in November 2010. He took 418 balls over his innings, an impressive strike rate of 66.50 runs per 100 balls.

"A flurry of boundaries as matters came to an end amply demonstrated De Villiers's complete and total superiority, as well as that of his side's," wrote Osman Samiuddin on the second day's play for Cricinfo. "In the second session he scored an even 100. Two overs after tea, as he deftly took a single to mid-wicket, Graeme Smith stood tallest and loudest in the dressing-room applauding as De Villiers went past his captain as holder of the highest individual Test score for South Africa. By then Pakistan were dead men walking." South Africa made 584 for nine declared; the match was drawn.

"I'd like to dedicate that knock to Graeme," said De Villiers afterwards. "He showed a lot of class in his captaincy by allowing me to go through and to get that record. I thought we could have declared a bit earlier, but he wanted me to push on and to get that record. I never expected to reach this kind of record. I did start believing when I got my double-hundred in India a couple of years ago, that's definitely when the belief started, but before then there was no hope at all. I was just playing the game for the fun of it and hoping to get a hundred here and there. The mindset has changed quite a bit and I do know now that I'm capable of scoring big runs and hopefully I will maintain that kind of form."

Another important big hundred was against Australia at Newlands in March 2009.

Australia made 209, and South Africa replied with 651 all out – their biggest total against Australia, beating the 622 for nine declared at Durban in 1969–70. De Villiers made 163 in only 196 balls, and South Africa went on to win by an innings and 20 runs.

It was Australia's first innings defeat in a decade, since March 1998 against India.

"De Villiers flogged a wilting attack in brilliant fashion," wrote *Wisden*. "A calculated assault on McDonald brought him four (all to leg) sixes off consecutive balls, making him the third batsman to achieve this feat in Test cricket after Kapil Dev and Shahid Afridi. De Villiers's two previous scoring shots had been sixes off McGain; he hit seven in all, as well as 12 fours. His buccaneering seventh wicket stand of 124 with Morkel took only 20 overs, and ensured South Africa would reach 651. The 62 extras were also the most conceded by Australia in any Test innings."

Ali put it to De Villiers that he is always visibly confident at the crease, enthusiastic and bustling and restless. "I enjoy showing visible energy at the crease," he agreed. "I've worked it out over ten years – that's what makes me a better player, and what works for me. It doesn't work for a player like Jacques Kallis to go running around like I do – but I know if I don't have that kind of energy, that body language, that confidence, then I'm not going to do well. I have observed and learned from my mistakes. I can't be calm at the wicket like a Kallis, it doesn't work for me. I like to show the opposition with my body language: if you don't get me out, I'm winning the game here."

Who was the best bowler he ever faced?

"I've always said Andrew Flintoff of England, and that's still probably the case. His stats don't say that he's one of the best ever, and he's had only one or two 'five-fors' in his career, but he was such a big-match player. I somehow always seemed to be up against him when the game was on the line. I remember at Edgbaston in August 2008, when we were batting to win the series and Graeme got 154 not out. I came in at the match-breaking moment, and I had to face Flintoff."

De Villiers made 27 that day, in a nerve-racking 97 minutes; he survived Flintoff, who had trapped both Neil McKenzie and Kallis lbw, but was caught off the spinner Monty Panesar. Mark Boucher (45) then stayed with Smith to see South Africa to a famous victory.

"Flintoff was unstoppable in that match," remembers De Villiers. "He almost won the game for them. Of course I did play against him when I was younger, and that could have something to do with how impressed I was by him." De Villiers scored 91 out of 206 when Johnson took seven for 68 at Centurion in 2014. He scored 43 of the runs Johnson conceded off 50 balls faced.

What about Mitchell Johnson? "Johnson is quick, but I felt I got the better of him. I don't want to sound arrogant, but I'm not scared of facing him. Of course he could get me out again in the future, and he's uncomfortable for the batsman. But when you play each other so often, you either become a buddy with a bowler like Mitchell or you get on top of him. I feel I'm on top of him."

Ali recalled the Adelaide Test in November 2012, when South Africa went into the last day on 77 for four, still needing 353 to win the match. A win was out of the question, but could South Africa somehow bat all day for a draw?

De Villiers batted more than four hours for 33 runs, which he scored off 220 balls. He put on 89 priceless runs with Faf du Plessis, who batted all day and made 110 not out off 376 balls. Kallis took over when De Villiers was out, and he and Du Plessis used up another two and a half hours together. South Africa finished on 248 for eight: only in Test cricket could a draw have been so exciting.

How did they survive? "I really enjoyed that Test match for exactly that reason," says De Villiers, "because I was able to show I'm not just a one-dimensional player who has to score at a run a ball. We were catching a lot of abuse on the field and then in the media, about how we were playing the game, how 'negative' we were. I just knew we had to guts it out – and that the momentum in a match can turn around very quickly. And it was great to bat so long with Faf – I've known him for a very long time. We were in the same class at school, both boarders, side by side all the way."

In the next Test at Perth, South Africa led by 62 runs on the first innings – and then smashed the Australian bowling in the second innings to set up a massive 309-run victory. De Villiers made 169 in 184 balls, the complete opposite of his painstaking 33 at Adelaide. "Those two Tests were two of the most enjoyable matches I've played in – going through all that pain and saving the game at Adelaide, and then completely dominating the Aussies at Perth. There was a lot of pleasure in that. We were scoring at over seven runs an over at one stage. We showed the whole world that we are an adaptable team, and that we can do anything. It's probably our biggest strength – how we can turn things around from any situation."

What ambitions does he still have in the game?

"It's never been about myself. I don't like talking about statistics. They're a nice reference point and I'll probably look back to my stats one day. But while I'm playing, it's been a pet hate of mine, people talking about stats. I just think that is missing the plot. There's nothing more rewarding than being a member of a winning team, and having a big influence on your mates around you … seeing youngsters grow into great cricket players, and knowing that you've had an influence on them. It would be nice to bring back a World Cup – but there's a bigger picture than just the World Cup."

Ali suggested that the 20-over game should be banned at school level, because it encourages players to hit out recklessly before they have learned to build an innings. "Whether we like it or not," De Villiers says, "it's become part of cricket now. Financially it's good for players and the organisers. There's way too much of T20, but there is a place for it. They've just got to find the balance – they're going too hard at the market at the moment.

"I make it look like I'm enjoying T20, but I'm really uncomfortable, feeling forced to bat hard from the very first over. More often than not, you're uncomfortable in that situation and you have to take risks. I believe the most successful players in T20 are still the conventional players, guys who set it up and take 10 or 12 balls to settle in, trying a make a run a ball. Whatever the format, you need to keep it simple, keeping your head still, trying to play the ball late."

In mid-2015, De Villiers is first in the ODI world rankings and third in the Test rankings. He is just 31 years old, with several years of batting ahead of him – and perhaps the best is yet to come.

Already he has passed 150 nine times in Tests, including two double-centuries. Against the West Indies in 2014–15 in South Africa, he scored 559 runs in six innings in ODIs and Tests – an average of 93.16 across both forms of the game.

In ODIs, he has a strike rate of 99.12, the best bar one of any batsman in history who has scored more than 2 000 runs and has an average higher than 35. His only rival among the major bats-men is Virender Sehwag (strike rate 104.33), but Sehwag averages 35.03 to De Villiers's 53.65. Only seven batsmen have achieved an ODI average above 50, and on that list De Villiers is second only to Hashim Amla (55.26). In fact they are the only two batsmen who have averaged more than 50 in both ODIs and Tests.

Ali mentioned to De Villiers the attitude of the West Indian Brian Lara: "His philosophy was that he wanted to dictate to the bowlers from the first ball. Viv Richards was like that, so was Graeme Pollock. I've seen you play shots that are amazing. I'll tell you straight, you are the most innovative batsman I have ever seen. Is this a result of work done in practice? Do you think about it at night? Are those fantastic shots spontaneous?"

"You talk about Brian Lara dictating … it's really about getting an understanding of the rhythm of a game. I talk to the team about it quite often. I believe that's what cricket is all about, as a team and as an individual. I've had the ability, from an early age, to sense a bit of weakness in the opposition, especially in bowlers. You can sense when your opponents don't have a lot of energy in the field.

"I think that's my biggest strength, I really do. I'd like to call it instinct, reading the situation really well. Hardly ever have I gone in from the first ball and thought, 'Well, today's the day and I'm really going to murder them.' I've always believed it's important to give it a bit of time and get a feel for what's going on. I manipulate really well for a while, and then I'll know when it's time to dominate.

"The shots I play are not practised deliberately in the nets ... but I am very structured in the way I practise. I do practise hard. I've got my little drills I go through. But those shots I play in the match, I work out on the day. I try to get a feel for what the opposing captain is trying to do, and play my shots accordingly to get round him.

"That's the important thing for any player to find out – what it is that sets you apart, makes you better than the rest. If you don't find that out, you are never going to be better than the rest."

AB de Villiers
Born 17 February 1984
International career: 2004–2015

	M	Inns	NO	Runs	HS	Avg	SR	100	50	Conv
Tests	98	162	16	7606	278*	52.09	54	21	36	36.84
First-class	124	207	21	9493	278*	51.03	56	24	50	32.43
ODIs	187	179	31	7941	162*	53.65	99	20	46	30.30
List A	219	210	34	9278	162*	52.71	97	23	55	29.48

As at 20 July 2015

POSTSCRIPT

So Who Is the
Greatest of the Great?

In October 2013, Ali Bacher wrote an article for The Cricketer *magazine to answer the question* Who is South Africa's greatest batsman? *In the event, the article was never published, but Ali stands by the view he expressed when he answered this notoriously difficult question. He also acknowledges that when modern players like AB de Villiers and Hashim Amla retire, they will also be judged by history as being among the greatest batsmen of all time.*

Before his untimely death, Bob Woolmer went public: "Jacques Kallis is South Africa's best ever batsman." Better than Graeme Pollock and Barry Richards? Shortly thereafter, media reports indicated that Kepler Wessels concurred with Bob's views. What are my views?

Graeme Pollock was destined for greatness even in his teens. At 16 he became the youngest South African to score a first-class century. At 19 he was the youngest South African to score a double-century in first-class cricket – 209 not out against the International Cavaliers in Port Elizabeth, against an attack that included Richie Benaud and Graham McKenzie.

Nobody punished a bad ball better than Graeme. His placement was superb and his trademark shot was the cover drive, which he would hit on the up with power, superb timing and grace. The only time I saw bowlers get the better of him was during the first four Tests in South Africa during the 1964-65 series against England. Fred Titmus and David Allen bowled straight at his middle stump, curbed his brilliant off-side strokes and dismissed him five times.

That dominance was short lived. Graeme developed a powerful pull shot and an on-drive, and in the fifth Test Graeme had the last laugh, scoring 137 and 77 not out. He gave enormous pleasure and excitement to the cricket-loving public, because his hundreds would be scored quickly – in 120 to 140 minutes – and would generally change the direction on any particular match.

His Test average of 60.97 remains second only to Sir Donald Bradman, an extraordinary achievement. I met the Don for the first time at his home in Adelaide in 1992. I asked him how good was Graeme. He said, "The best left-hander of all time." I said, "Better than Garry Sobers?" He said, "Yes, although marginally, and obviously Garry is the greatest all-rounder of all time."

Jacques Kallis was also destined in his teens to be great. When he was 15 I received a call from Cape Town. I was told a future batting star had been identified at Wynberg Boys' High School. I always thought Colin Cowdrey had the best batting technique of all the batsmen I played against, then came Barry Richards and his was better, and finally Jacques Kallis. probably had the best of all of them. That is the reason he never had a long bad trot.

He is mentally very strong. The Aussies tried to break him. He revealed his big-match temperament in his seventh Test in Melbourne in 1997, when he scored his maiden Test century. The Melbourne Cricket Ground holds 100 000 people but it was pretty empty on that Monday. It was extraordinary, the acoustics – whatever the players said, you could hear in the stands. I can see and hear it as if it was yesterday. Michael Kasprowicz bowling to Jacques, loud-mouthing and verbalising him. But he never flinched. Eventually, Kasprowicz bowled a bouncer without effect, and verbalised him again. Finally, beyond frustrated, Kasprowicz said, "Is this man fucking deaf?"

Mike Procter used to say that in one aspect of batting, Brian Lara and Sachin Tendulkar had the edge on Jacques. They could dominate attacks far more freely. But Jacques will tell you that, for most of his Test career, our strength was our fast bowlers and not our batting, and he was thus forced to become our rock, our pillar within our batting line-up. Sadly he is only now in South Africa being acknowledged for his greatness. I interviewed Steve Waugh recently for TV. I asked him how good was Kallis. He said, "One of the greatest cricketers of all time."

Barry Richards unfortunately played only four Tests but how good was he? I asked this question when I met Sir Donald Bradman. He said, "He was as good as Sir Jack Hobbs and Sir Leonard Hutton." Enough said. One of the greatest batting performances ever was by Barry Richards playing for South Australia against Western Australia, at the WACA ground in Perth during November 1970, and hardly a South African is aware of the following story.

At the close of play on day one, South Australia were 513 for three, and Barry had 325 not out. He had gone from 79 to 216 between lunch and tea, and from 216 to 325 after tea. He was eventually out for 356, scored off 381 balls, and was at the crease for 372 minutes. The bowlers in the Western Australia attack were Test class – none other than the great Dennis Lillee, the formidable Graeme McKenzie and the experienced Tony Lock.

Barry had an uncanny cricket brain. In 1970 Bill Lawry's Aussie team toured South Africa. They had a mystery flick-spin bowler named Johnny Gleeson. The first time we faced him was day one of the first Test at Newlands and he mesmerised all of our batsmen that day except for Barry. We had a team meeting that evening. After a short stint at the wicket, Barry had him worked out. If you saw a lot of fingers over the ball, it was the leg-break; and if you saw the ball between thumb and forefinger, it was the off-break. Gleeson was their best bowler and never once got Barry out in the series. I always tell Barry that my finest batting achievement was to keep him out of our Test team against Bobby Simpson's Australians in 1966–67. Sadly, again, he has never been acknowledged in South Africa for his greatness.

So who is the best of these great batsmen?

After much serious consideration, I am going to gently nudge Barry Richards ahead – by a hair's breadth. Why? He is the most complete all-round batsman I have seen. He opened the batting, and that position has to be the most difficult of all the different batting positions.

Acknowledgements

The following people helped in the preparation and completion of this book, and warm thanks are extended to them:

Colin Bland, Graeme Pollock, Barry Richards, Gary Kirsten, Jacques Kallis, Graeme Smith, Kevin Pietersen, AB de Villiers and Hashim Amla kindly agreed to be interviewed by Ali, and provided much new information about their careers and experiences.

Andrew Samson, the world's leading cricket statistician, for his exhaustive checking of the statistics and, no less important, the insights he provided in the interpretation of the numbers. Any errors in transcribing his contributions and corrections are our responsibility.

Krish Reddy provided vital information on great black cricketers who did not get the opportunity to compete at official international level. Krish is an honours graduate in English from the University of Durban Westville and a retired school principal. He has written numerous articles on black cricket in national newspapers and magazines. Krish has painstakingly recovered many of the lost statistical records of black and non-racial cricket in Natal and South Africa. He is the author of several pioneering books on black cricket. In December 2003, to mark their 50th year of publication, the Mutual & Federal SA Cricket Annual honoured him "for the accurate recording of the deeds of generations of cricketers". He was chosen in 2007 as Statistician of the Year by the UK-based Association for Cricket Statisticians and Historians.

The team at Penguin Random House, especially Robert Plummer and Janet Bartlet.

Alison Lowry: her editing was as always impeccable, her encouragement in tough times inspirational.

Pam Thornley, for her meticulous proofreading of the text.

Tim Hutchinson, executive chairman of Douglas Green, for his ready enthusiasm, generosity and attention to detail in employing the Boschendal brand to assist with the launch of the book.

ALI BACHER
DAVID WILLIAMS
JULY 2015

Note on Sources
and Bibliography

Sources

The main source of information and contemporary reporting was the *Wisden Cricketers' Almanack* for all the relevant years, either in book form or through the website www.espncricinfo.com, which offers ready and flexible access to an astonishing range and depth of statistics, scorecards, information and match reports. Another extremely useful website was www.cricketarchive.com.

Unless otherwise stated, the quotations used in the book are drawn from *Wisden* or espncricinfo.com, or from recorded interviews conducted by Ali Bacher in 2014 and 2015.

Select bibliography

Luke Alfred, *Testing Times: The Story of the Men Who Made SA Cricket* (Spearhead, 2003)

David Rayvern Allen (editor), *A Word from Arlott: A collection of John Arlott's broadcasts, cricket commentaries and writings* (Pelham Books, 1983)

John Arlott, *John Arlott's 100 Greatest Batsmen* (Macdonald Queen Anne Press, 1986)

Norman Barrett, *The Daily Telegraph Chronicle of Cricket* (Guinness, 1994)

Sir Donald Bradman, *The Art of Cricket* (Hodder & Stoughton, 1984)

Jack Cheetham, *I Declare* (Howard Timmins, 1956)

Michael Davie and Simon Davie, *The Faber Book of Cricket* (Faber & Faber, 1987)

Ted Dexter, *Ted Dexter Declares: An Autobiography* (Stanley Paul, 1966)

Louis Duffus, *Cricketers of the Veld* (Sampson Low, 1947)

——, *South African Cricket 1927–1947* (SA Cricket Association/CAN, 1948)

Benny Green (editor), *The Concise Wisden: An Illustrated Anthology of 125 Years* (Macdonald Queen Anne Press, 1988)

—— (editor), *The Wisden Book of Obituaries* (Macdonald Queen Anne Press, 1986)

Rodney Hartman, *Ali: The Life of Ali Bacher* (Penguin Books, 2006)

Christopher Lane (editor), *A Century of Wisden* (John Wisden, 2000)

Jackie McGlew and Trevor Chesterfield, *South Africa's Cricket Captains: From Melville to Wessels* (Southern Books, 1994)

Bruce Murray and Christopher Merrett, *Race and Politics in Springbok Cricket* (Wits University Press/University of KwaZulu-Natal Press, 2004)

Barry Richards, *The Barry Richards Story* (Faber, 1978)

RS Whitington, *Simpson's Safari: South African Test Series 1966–67* (Howard Timmins, 1967)

Wisden Cricketers' Almanack, selected annual editions from 1896 to 2012

Index

Page numbers referring to photographs are indicated in **bold**.